PHOENIX MUSIC GUIDES: 1

Concerto

PHOENIX MUSIC GUIDES: 1

CONCERTO

PERCY M. YOUNG

M.A., MUS.D.

WITH ELEVEN DRAWINGS BY

MILEIN COSMAN

PHOENIX HOUSE LTD

LONDON

'*Whatever helps to maintain the common society of men, or whatever brings it about that men live together in peace and agreement, is useful . . .*'

Spinoza, *Ethics*, Pt IV Prop. XL

Printed in Great Britain
in 10/12 point Monotype Garamond by
The Bowering Press of Plymouth for
Phoenix House Ltd, 38 William IV Street,
Charing Cross, W.C.2
First Published 1957

785.6
Y7

Contents

Introduction, 7

21115

Most of the illustrations in this book were
specially drawn by Miss Cosman, but those
appearing on pages 11, 67, 127 and 145 are
reproduced by kind permission of
The Radio Times

INTRODUCTION

IT IS NOT, perhaps, out of place to refer the reader to the old saw that beauty is in the eye of the beholder. For it is—or should be—axiomatic that appreciation of the fine arts is a personal, private matter; and happy is he who, steering clear of faction and fashion, can form his own conclusions as to what is, and what is not, significant. But where to begin?

The first aim of the *Phoenix Music Guides* is to make suggestions in this respect, by setting out a representative exhibition comprising most of the works that belong to the general repertoire and some which may be less familiar but which are generally available through recorded performance. Having done this some attempt is made to explain the character of the different provinces of music; in this case of *Concerto*.

What is a Concerto? How do concertos come to be written? Thus far we may proceed by way of the factual; by rehearsing history, and by displaying some formal structures. Neither history nor form, however, is an end in itself; for the meaning of music lies well beyond the limits of scientific knowledge. That the more we know about music the greater our understanding is at most but half a truth.

The idea that a musical work has a fixed 'meaning' tends sometimes to become obsessional, and it is part of the present project to try to remove this obsession by returning the reader to his own capacity for observation. This is the ultimate key to 'meaning'. Each of us has a natural approach to music in that some aspects (discussed at length in the first chapter) are more evident than others. But awareness of other attitudes extends our own field of observation, and helps to deepen perception. Thus standards of judgment are established, and from early contentment with 'liking' music the listener moves to a second stage—of 'appreciation'.

Whoever it was who claimed architecture to be 'frozen music' gave a useful lead; for there is a homogeneity in the arts, derived from the common purpose to institute order out of chaos. Any hints which relate to the other arts should, I think, be followed up. For by reference now to painting, now to architecture, now to literature, or to whatever accomplishment in which the listener has experience, the patterns of music take such significance that they become explicable. It is, of course, not necessary to be able to talk about music; but it assists confidence in judgment and the sociability that music engenders. Some of my younger friends, I notice, are ready to discuss music—but in the language of the text-book, from which they obtain the opinions that are permissible. Later on they tend to follow, rather too slavishly, the reactions of more or less distinguished critics. Independence in expression is a matter of some importance and should be encouraged.[1]

A rough estimate shows that there is a constant one per cent of the community in Britain devoted to music of the order described in these books. Of this number I am reminded of the considerable majority whose acquaintance with music stops short of practical achievement, and to whom the printed note is often not communicative. There are, therefore, no musical examples herein. On the other hand there are a good many hints that investment in miniature scores (see the Index of Works) is a sound proposition. Not infrequently there are references in this book to detailed sections of scores, so that the keen reader may see what he hears in relation to its context. It is remarkable how much the eye will be found to help the ear, and some spadework in score-reading will often be both revealing and rewarding.

[1] Cf., the findings and conclusions of *Poetry and Children* (Methuen, 1956).

So we buy (or borrow) records and scores. But, maybe, we want to 'know something about the composer'. Then we pursue biography together with some detailed musical exegesis through the companionable volumes of Messrs Dent's *Master Musicians* series. To such reading this volume and its successors are intended as preparatory. Gazetteers rather than text-books, they indicate to the amateur of music what points of special interest he might perceive in certain types of music, or, in some cases, in individual works. To 'analyse' each work is neither practicable nor desirable. But those for whom this is an important occupation (i.e. examination candidates) will find sufficient to enable them hereafter to do their own dissections, which is much better than having the work done for them.

There are, said my publisher, a lot of people who listen to music who cannot read it nor yet understand, or are impatient with, the manner in which it is sometimes written about. For them this book is intended as a finger-post to the enlargement of their musical experience.

P. M. Y.

I. On Perceptive Listening

❡ TOWARDS UNDERSTANDING · In theory there is no good reason why the ear should be thought of as an organ of sense inferior to the eye; but, commonly, it is so considered, and the limits of reality are assumed firmly to be set within visual range. Hence the coming of television has proved a blessing to those whose enjoyment of radio was tempered by an inability to discipline the roving eye. Seeing, after all, is believing.

If one can touch what one sees—or if what one sees can appear to be palpably touchable—then there is even greater confidence that the 'real thing' is present. So we are aware of the reason for the most recent technical developments within the cinema. And so, up to a point, we become aware of the apparent remoteness of what is generically termed 'modern music'. The disdain which sometimes accompanies this term is an admission of incapacity in understanding an art which, evading illusions of visibility or tangibility, is the antithesis of 3D. To the materialist all music must appear as tiresome, for its essence lies in having no substantial existence.

Yet there is this paradox: that music was never before so much and so widely desired as at the present time. At the moment we may forget the arbitrary rulings which grade music-lovers into various classes of appreciative distinction—like exhibits in a flower show; for it is not immediately to the point whether the enthusiast in the queue is after a ticket for a performance by Louis Armstrong or Eileen Joyce. What is worth consideration is the inclination towards exploring the unknown; even though the individual may delude himself that all that he desires is what is already familiar.

He who would appreciate (as he says) music is, necessarily, constrained to reflection on what is not there. Of a symphony, a concerto, a sonata we can only refer to what was; for the whole work exists only after its performance has ended.

Thus we arrive at the crux of the matter: memory. The memory is stored with what, in this instance, we have heard. The ability to judge what we have heard, to consider it in relation to similar or dissimilar experiences, or in relation to ideas which may indeed not lie solely within the field of music, depends on acute listening. This, then, is the foundation of musical understanding.

No two of us, however, listen to music in the same way. This, I may say, is the chord of C major. To some it is just that—a fixed sound with major third and perfect fifth superimposed. To others, indifferent to acoustical detail, it is a familiar, practical detail, encountered in the performance of music. Or, because of unconscious associations, the chord of C major may generate hope, just as the complementary chord of C minor may suggest the reverse. We shall, ultimately, learn how the craft of composition directs the material of music into logical modes of expression; but in apprehension there will always be disparities, which are due to differences of approach. We must, therefore, commence with the premise that no two listeners will agree on the particulars of musical significance.

It may be argued that the more the listener knows about

music—which generally implies what he knows of the technique of music—the greater will be his enjoyment. This may be, but is not necessarily, the case.

⟨ SOME LISTENING HABITS · By way of experiment a representative group of concert-goers was consulted as to individual habits of listening.

The music student, well aware of the various structural forms of music, listened so that he might appreciate the construction of music: the text-books, he implied, suggested that this was a proper route to musical wisdom. The surgeon, an amateur oboist, concentrated on the tone quality of instruments or voices, and found his greatest satisfaction in the tone values of separate instruments or concerted groups; at the same time he considered the quality of performance. Oddly, however, he was aware of other, more inaccessible factors so that while he derived great pleasure from the performance of certain music he disliked the music itself. An amateur violinist was content to follow the orchestral line of the first violins. Three sheet-metal workers (whose experience was primarily in 'jazz', but whose evidence was none the less valuable) respectively acknowledged first interest in the instruments (vibraphone, saxophone, and brass specifically); the rhythm; and the emotional content of music. A young engineer found that the 'character' of any musical work reflected the character of the composer: thus, in particular, he apprehended, he thought, Sibelius the man through his symphonies. A lady of middle age, and zealous concert-going habits, confessed to building up within her imagination visual images in accordance with the supposed intention of the composer.

This catalogue is capable of infinite expansion, but some conclusions will not be altered.

⟨ SENSIBILITY · Each approach to music as already described is a valid approach and yields some measure of aesthetic or emotional satisfaction that admittedly could be derived from no other source. But it is clear that, as two heads are better than one, a combination of attitudes towards musical perception should prove rewarding. What we are looking for becomes evident when we know *how* to look, or, in this case, listen. And how to listen is shown by general experience. What follows is a synthesis of common methods of listening, and the primary aim is to enlarge sensibility rather than to increase factual knowledge.

⁋ THE COMMONPLACE · The miracle of great art lies in the transformation of the commonplace, and the beginning of true appreciation comes when Shelley's phrase that 'poetry . . . makes familiar objects be as if they were not familiar', rings true. The foundation of all musical works is inevitably familiar. Even the most venturesome dodecaphonalist can only manipulate his thoughts within the limits of the twelve semitones of a chromatic scale. In the music of Beethoven and Bach, Mozart and Haydn, the most sublime patterns evolved from sections of scales, or artless arpeggios, such as furnish sight-reading exercises for children in junior schools.

The opening of the 'Eroica' symphony, of the 'Gratias agimus' in the Mass in B Minor, of the 'Haffner' symphony, of the slow movement of the 'Surprise' symphony: all these are commonplace. Yet they are all germinal. In each movement the *incipit* returns in different guises.

Consciously to follow the behaviour of such melodic points through a score is an invigorating discipline (when conscious effort is made all extraneous thoughts are excluded), which immediately brings awareness of some of the conditions of logic and imagination applicable to music. A movement has, of course, a diversity of melody—but at the outset to concentrate on the behaviour of one is enough. When quickly to grasp significant melodic shapes, and to recognize the variation to which inevitably they are submitted in the course of musical argument, becomes a habit the relative importance of various themes will also become apparent. Melody, however, is more than pitch. It is also rhythm. In this respect Beethoven especially is our exemplar. Consider the opening movement of the third pianoforte concerto, and of the violin concerto, in both of which the ground-swell of the music is a rhythmic impulse.

⁋ RELATIONSHIPS · By noticing the single factor we become aware of relationships; between one theme and another, between one chord and another, between one instrument and another. In orchestral music the obvious relationships suggest the quality of spaciousness as a distinguishing feature. The world of the orchestra, it is felt, is a large world.

The difference between the sounds of piccolo and double-bassoon may be defined mathematically, but in general we prefer a definition by analogy. Thus we feel, and say, that between the *high* sound of the one and the *low* sound of the other there is a great *distance*. So much do we feel that music has a quasi-geographical existence that we invariably add 'contour' to the terminology. In short, whether we wish it or not, the visual sense inescapably plays its part in musical perception.

Ultimately the trained eye can, in fact, translate the visual symbols of music (the notes of a score) into aural symbols, and it becomes possible—up to a point—to read a score, as a book, with some notion of the *physical* effect—in short, one can hear what one sees. This, maybe, is an occupation for a specialist, but the music-lover may go some way in this direction. Working backwards it can be felt that the sounds of music as organized within a work assemble into an area of lines and colours: the resultant impression may at first be indeterminate, but by careful focussing a more precise impression may eventually be formed. Herein we are helped by the lay-out of the concert platform. The violins are here, the violas there, the cellos and basses in their ordered cohorts. Each department of the orchestra may be *seen* to add its contribution to the music in progress.

❦ THE SCORE · An orchestral score is a fascinating document. It is the record of work to be done by each member of the orchestra, as well as the outward sign of creative imagination. It is the point at which the past—the moment of inspiration—combines with the present—the listener's appreciation. It is a form of document with which the music-lover might well become acquainted; and on the whole more intelligible, because less ambiguous, than, say, an income tax return. At the outset the earnest, but untutored, music-lover is urged to add to his library a miniature score of some work by Mozart.

The first page of Mozart's concerto in A major (K. 488) for pianoforte and orchestra shows modest requirements: a flute, two clarinets, and two bassoons comprise the woodwind section; the brass are represented only by two horns. Then, separating the wind from the strings (this work dispenses entirely with percussion), are the two staves allocated to the pianoforte. The bottom of the page is occupied by the two violin groups (each with a separate stave), and the violas, cellos, and double basses.

For eight bars of this score only the strings are employed. For the succeeding four bars it is the turn of the wind. Throughout the score it is clear that there are many opportunities for players to listen to their colleagues—a characteristic of 'classical' instrumentation. Sometimes a bassoon, or a flute, or the pair of clarinets demand special attention. Variety is apparent from the *look* of the music. In listening to the same music the sounds, seemingly transferred from the printed score to the blank page of the imagination which is taken to each performance, are experienced as emblems of orderly thought.

On the whole, however, I am not one for sending every neophyte to Promenade Concerts score in hand. The thing to do is to browse among scores as among books, to look at them in private together with radio or gramophone, or even without either. (The student proper, of course, will try his hand at transferring scores to the piano keyboard.) There are details which at first will not signify, but these can wait. What we begin to acquire is a sense of direction. A traveller carries a map in his hand (he may have another in his pocket); a concert-goer, who is another sort of traveller—remembering Keats's 'realms of gold'— another sort of map.

❲ COLOUR · Once the idea of space is accepted that of colour becomes inevitable. The distinctive timbre of an instrument (or voice) affects the ear as colour affects the eye, for thereby the lines of melody appear to acquire more notable character. The point might also be made that application of the inapt timbre may well destroy every vestige of character: there is, for example, barely a tune which will survive a shaky overlay of cornet or saxophone.

A glance at an orchestral score gives advance information about the general colour scheme. Comparison between the Mozart score detailed above with, say, one of the Tchaikovsky concertos will be found to make a helpful preliminary exercise to the hearing of either, or both. Or let us compare two works by the same composer in this respect. In his first pianoforte and violin concertos Tchaikovsky uses in the main the same orchestra. But there is one major addition to the former score. The trombones are present. Their characteristic tone quality is unmistakable and its presence in the score is in keeping with the general powerful urge of this particular concerto. In the slow movement, *andantino semplice*, of the concerto there is a fine example of the colour potential of the trombones. In the whole movement they are permitted to blow only one quaver chord. That is, apparently, short commons; but the effect on normal ears is near cataclysmic.

To know the personality of musical instruments is one way to avoid the musical equivalent of colour-blindness. Mr Britten's *Young Person's Guide to the Orchestra* is an exhilarating introduction to the complete orchestral family; but those who like to make friends more or less gradually may prefer to follow the fortunes of the various instruments in a quieter manner. (One can mark obvious solo passages in a score with red or green ink, put on the record, and then wait for the particular moment of discovery.) But, after all, this is a book about concertos, and before we come to the end we shall have discovered a concerto for practically every civilized instrument, as well as some that are barely so.

The relationship of instrument to instrument provokes the analogy of colour, but so also can the relationship of note to note, or chord to chord. This, we may say, taking any one of the top half-dozen notes on the piano, is 'bright'; but, turning to one of the lowest, that is 'dark'. There is no change of instrument but there is, apparently, of character. Seven bars from the end of the slow movement of Tchaikovsky's first piano concerto the piano part contains two separate harmonic statements, one of D flat major, the other of A major. These contrasted chords, whether recognized quite precisely for what they are or not, show, simply, how kaleidoscopic music may appear within its own limits and unaffected by changes of timbre.

Using the eye to assist the ear is important not only because

B

music thereby appears more purposeful, but also because the possible analogies combat any sense of remoteness. There is, after all, very little difference between our apperception of the visible and the audible, for both are communicated by wave motion, the one of light, the other of sound. In reverse, we may note the sensibility of the sightless to sounds; the blind learn to see with their ears.

To give a direct and definitive answer to the frequent question 'what is the music about?' is impossible. Up to this point, however, it has been shown that it is possible to demonstrate the kind of music: how we have certain patterns and certain colours. We may proceed further than this and say that the nature of these patterns and colours is, in large part, due to environment.

⟪ ENVIRONMENT · Handel's orchestra differs from that of Mozart, while his, in turn, is not that of Brahms. Each composer betrays his presence by certain unmistakable gestures, or characteristics. So we may begin to recognize that period and place have their effect on music. Mozart's music is symbolic, at many times, of the aristocratic principle which was strongly held by many during the eighteenth century. Tchaikovsky's music has more in it of what we might consider to be democratic. This is by no means to suggest that the music of one is of necessity greater than the music of the other, but merely to advance the theory that points of view, or conditions of culture, can—often unconsciously—be reflected in music.

A neat and orderly mind no doubt enjoys the classification of art, and the recognition of such class divisions as place and period suggest.

In proposing that the date at which a work was composed might show in the work we approach rather close to possible concepts of reality. The eighteenth-century quality of Handel, however, is not the essence of Handel's music, but it extends towards the essential idea, of which what we hear is the outward sign. Experience tends to prove, however, that recognition of outer qualities may well lead to a perception of inner virtues. Appreciation of art is a matter of relativity. The masterpiece is so assessed after consideration of other works; but intrinsically it carries an absolute quality. It is this which confers immortality and which, to the artist philosopher, represents truth.

⟨ PHILOSOPHY · Progress towards this ideal—it was adequately defined by Plato in the *Symposium*—is the end of the career of the music-lover. It should be said, however, that the end of the career is never reached. That is why music is especially honoured in heaven.

Now music differs from the other arts in that its existence demands some large measure of re-creation on the part of the listener. It is necessary, so to speak, to be within the music. The technical expert (like my student whose capacity for 'formal analysis' is considerable) is at a disadvantage, for he is liable to mistrust the intuitive and, by aiming at objectivity, to isolate himself from the living quality. The relatively untutored amateur— without abnormal prejudice—has one advantage in being able to associate himself more intimately with the musical experience. Music, he recognizes, is a 'change'. Because it is a 'change' he sometimes experiences a sense of guilt, being afraid of the label 'escapist'.

This term is misunderstood, and grotesquely misapplied. The concert-goer escapes—that is, frees himself from—the presence of the mundane. But he in no sense enters a vacuum, a state of nothing. The matter of 'reality' is sometimes obsessive. It is possible, though there is no substance for the hypothesis, that Handel *père* suggested to the young George Frideric that he should quit daydreaming and advance himself in the law so that he might be of some *practical* significance in the world. Handel might well have made an excellent advocate, but such a career could have shown nothing more 'real' than his actual achievements.

There is a point in this presentation of diverse occupations: the lawyer and the composer. For law and order are common to both. In his *Chronicle of My Life* Stravinsky underlines this: 'The phenomenon of music is given to us with the sole purpose of establishing an order in things, including, and particularly, the co-ordination between *man* and *time*'. Therein, perhaps, is vindication (if justification be needed) of the art against the charge of 'unreality'.

❡ EYE AND EAR · Ultimately it is discovered that aids to appreciation which were once helpful are no longer so. 'Programme' music, with its literary connotations, is a delight to some insofar as it helps, in palatable terms, to create interest in the composer's design. Its provenance is always a matter of interest also, because it relates to the composer's extra-mural interests, and one feels thereby a familiarity with him—which is an additional aid to musical understanding. But once the premise of 'orderliness' is accepted there are no barriers to an equality of appreciation in both 'programme' and 'absolute' music.

It was said in the pioneer days that radio would revolutionize musical appreciation. Up to a point this prophecy has been fulfilled. The popularity of musical programmes on television might lead to a new surge of optimism, among those who cultivate the missionary spirit. They are irrelevant to our present study, but those who are possessed of the fallacy that seeing music—in the sense of seeing the musicians—is slightly indecent need putting in their place. The fascination of the eye can well lead to the fascination of the ear, and while televised Castles in Spain do not necessarily improve the common understanding of Lalo's *Symphonie Espagnole* the admirable presentations of orchestral concerts (in which the camera follows the music player by player, and group by group) might. Again—seeing is believing.

Thus the orchestra on the platform, the pre-eminent soloist, and the conductor give some visual index to the quality and order of the music which they play.

There before our eyes is the dramatic nature of the concerto.

To sit on the side of the hall from which you may watch the pianist's fingers: from this point many experiences in music have taken flight.

II. What is a Concerto ?

¶ CONCERT · Some words have a nobility of their own. One such word is concert, and by the Utopian idea—Utopian, at least, at its first conception—of the Concert of Europe it is forever in a special category. That co-operation, the root of 'concert', should supplant conflict is as desirable in world affairs now as it was immediately after the Napoleonic Wars. Now concert precisely represents *concerto*, being the English way of putting the Italian; and in both languages the word has a general and a particular significance, the latter being within the field of music.

But how, it may be asked, can a *concerto* be a concert, when, at the same time, it can, and frequently is, part of a concert?

If, as is often urged, music is an incentive to clear and logical thought we seem to have made an inauspicious start. In fact we have not, but have come up against the habit of taking things for granted. By taking things for granted we impede our understanding of music.

'What is a concerto?' I asked three intelligent people. The first, unhesitatingly, gave the conventional answer: 'It is a piece for soloist with orchestral accompaniment.' The second, more cautious and with an eye on etymology, pensively murmured 'playing together'. The third catechumen was having no non-sense: 'It all depends. . . .'

A concerto, thanks to the publicity agents, may well appear as something played by a name set in six-inch lettering on a hand-bill, with some assistance from a supporting cast noted in rela-tively abject type. But the impression given is misleading, for there is not a member of a concerto-playing ensemble who cannot wreck a performance by wilfulness or incompetence. The Brahms violin concerto, in respect of its slow movement, is a corner in paradise; the oboist, however, has it in his power, by faulty intonation, by undue sentimentality, or by the mere inter-polation of wrong notes, to land the listener somewhat nearer to purgatory. What goes for the oboist goes too for the rest of the orchestra. The distinguished stranger who stands before them may be *primus*, but only *primus inter pares*: the first among equals.

❡ THE PLACE OF THE VIRTUOSO · There is nothing quite so salutary as the nonsense of Bernard Shaw in his erstwhile part of *Corno di Bassetto*. 'Concertos', he once wrote, 'should, on all ordinary occasions, be played by members of the orchestra, and not by wandering "stars" who pay an agent a lump sum to foist them off for three or six months on givers of concerts and parties as distinguished virtuosos. All masterpieces should be rehearsed up to that point of intimate knowledge which the Manchester band [conducted then by Sir Charles Hallé] has attained in its Berlioz repertoire.' Such practice, if more general, would, per-haps, reveal the wealth of music that lies under the generic term of concerto.

We do, of course, relish the spectacle of the virtuoso—in whatever field. Nor is virtuosity inimical to co-operation. The greatest virtuoso among modern statesmen was, of course, the most outstanding in his recognition of common ends. This ex-ample, moreover, reminds us that within co-operation there must also be conflict; that out of conflict the single purpose is achieved: or that all agreements must be agreements to differ on secondary issues. Of this the whole of great music is symbolic. Thus we are brought to a criterion of judgment. Music which has no con-flict is meaningless—even though its sensual effect may be satisfying—or stupefying. On the other hand, music which is all conflict without resolution is equally meaningless. It is, my bewildered friend says of a contemporary work,[1] all discord. If in truth this is the case (which it isn't) the music is bad: 'Why', wrote Browning, 'rush'd the discords in, but that harmony should be prized?'

My friend, however, misunderstands discord and concord, regarding both in a confined and technical sense. Discord may mean 'clashing sounds'—as roughnesses in chordal structure; but it may also mean 'variance', or 'disagreement' in a more general way. Harmony, as the chordal organization of music is narrowly called, is but one factor among many in the organization of music, and by no means the most important. Instrumental sonorities are far more evident, and discord, in a literal sense, is set up when any two instruments of different tone qualities are placed in apposition. Obviously instruments play co-operatively, in the sense that they obey the same timetable and the same key conditions in any one work (although in some modern works there are not uncommon examples of relaxation of these conditions); but the manner in which the instruments arrive at points of temporary supremacy is the result of musical effort and this it is that stimulates the intellectual interest of the listener.

The concerto which features a soloist is the supreme musical emblem of this aspect, and interpretation of that fundamental discord which is the origin of all art. No contest is quite so absorbing as one in which the individual is shown in conflict with the rest of the community, when the issues involved are of heroic proportions. In the concerto there unconsciously arises the identification of self with the musical protagonist. It is the ideal of musical experience that the listener should live through it, which means that he becomes absorbed in the action of the music. Concerto, because of the clarity of the tonal contrasts and the apparent contest of forces, lends itself immediately to this understanding. Hence the pleasure derived from this form of music, and its patent popularity.

⁋ THE DRAMATIC · At heart, then, the familiar type of concerto

[1] Ian Parrott's excellently taut *Pensieri*, a *concerto grosso* for string orchestra,

has a dramatic significance, and the display of solo virtuosity that is an essential part of the scheme enhances the dramatic element. A recognizable feature, indeed often the obvious distinguishing feature, of a concerto is the cadenza. At a certain point, or points, in the course of a concerto the orchestra may frequently be seen to leave the field clear for the soloist, who proceeds to a generally brilliant, lengthy, and private disquisition on tunes which have previously been prominent. This episode occurs as a rule towards the end of the first or last movement, or both. Herein the individual has full scope and the audience is all on his side, for here, indeed, is freedom for the one from the many.

In other days freedom not seldom became licence. The art of extempore playing is now out of fashion (except by church organists who still need to fill gaps in the liturgical routine). Originally, when the arts of composition and performance were not so widely separated as to-day, any singer or instrumentalist was capable of producing a gloss of his own on any text presented for his interpretation. In fact the great solo performers of the seventeenth and eighteenth centuries, armed with the comfortable knowledge that they could charge whatever fees they liked, insisted that any public appearance should entitle them to display to the full their particular qualities of execution.

❡ CADENZA · Concert-goers of previous generations were by no means so well-trained as now. Not for them the unbroken solemnity of three or four movements. Applause was frequent and interjectory. Testimonies to audience enthusiasm came both from Handel and Mendelssohn, who refer to the interruption of concertos by violent demonstrations after *cadenzas*. The *cadenza*, however, has retained its place in the general scheme of concertos and its treatment is always a matter for interest and speculation. It is a point in music where personality counts. The personality of the instrument, of course, but also the personality of the executant—as, for instance, in Brahms's violin concerto, where the *cadenza* was composed by Joachim, for whom the concerto was written; of the composer, as in Elgar's violin concerto; or of the editor. This latter functionary may easily be a menace. In a charming, light-weight concerto in B flat for cello

the editor of a certain edition takes ten minutes over an interpolated *cadenza*, which is intended primarily to show his learning
rather than to illuminate Boccherini's sprightly wit.

⁋ INDIVIDUALITY OF PERFORMER · In that a concerto is more
often than not designed for a specific performer the whole
character of the solo part will outline certain traits of executive
individuality. Vaughan Williams wrote a concerto-type piece for
Larry Adler, the mouth-organist, not so long ago. When Miss
Harriet Cohen damaged her right hand Sir Arnold Bax obliged
with a concerto for left hand. Not that he was the first thus to
restrict himself, for Ravel had also composed such a work. Viola
concertos by Walton and Bartók reflect the capacities of Tertis
and Primrose. Archie Camden, the bassoonist, has had concertos
for his instrument from Eric Fogg and Gordon Jacob.

Music of olden time recalls a ghostly company. In the violin
concerto of Brahms Joachim is abroad. In the clarinet and horn
concertos of Mozart Anton Stadler and Joseph Leutgeb are
memorialized. Mendelssohn's violin concerto is his epitome of
the musicianly personality of Ferdinand David. Beethoven's
pianoforte concertos are as they are because they represent his
attitude to the instrument, just as in Handel's organ concertos
we can appreciate the manner in which he played for the delectation of his patrons between the acts of his oratorios.

In short, just as plays are designed for the capacities of one
sort of player so are concertos for another. The result may be of
no more than temporary interest. This is when the dramatist or
the composer subordinates himself to the peculiar talents of his
exponent. On the other hand, a musical work may outlive its
progenitors. This happens when the relationship between soloist
and ensemble, between individual and the community, is balanced
and, therefore, relevant to all times; and is an aspect of the quality
defined as classical.

⁋ LIVING QUALITY OF MUSIC · There is a fallacy that what is old
is therefore classical. This is a fallacy from which the musical
pilgrim should rapidly escape, otherwise he will believe that
virtue and dullness are synonymous. Examples of early music
are awarded diplomas rather too frequently on account of their

age, usually before they are heard: the interpreter is zealous (or might be) for textural purity and frequently displays a judicial detachment. The audience, thinking on the easily apprehended rhapsodic and rhetorical characteristics of the late nineteenth century, allows to Bach, or Vivaldi, or Corelli the respect equal to that accorded to a Roman coin in a museum. The living quality is missed.

Each age, it should be remembered, has its own appreciation of what is dramatic; and a basic feeling for the dramatic was no less vital two centuries or more ago than at the present time. Thus the tonal contrasts in the concertos of Corelli as played in Rome at the beginning of the eighteenth century, or in the concertos of Bach composed for the Margrave of Brandenburg's private band, were in their own time appreciated as powerful expressions of dramatic thought.

One purpose of music is to move the listener emotionally. This is accomplished in the first place by the choice of voices or instruments. But the organization of the sounds produced calls for the manipulation of climax, and this, in turn, calls for design. Design in music is termed form, and the formal element, because it is readily analysable, tends to acquire an undue importance, insofar as the listener is concerned. When design is perfect whether in music, in poetry, in drama, in urban development, or in engineering, we accept it without comment: it is the absence of formal excellence that is noticeable.

⟦ ELEMENTS OF DESIGN · Formal habits change little. We are still attracted to the principles of duality and trinity. Music is recognized as fast or slow. We have, therefore, fast movements and slow movements. The contrast between such movements admits a dramatic factor into the design of large-scale works. To return to our original question as to the constitution of a concerto we now add the observation that most concertos within common experience have three movements: quick, slow, quick.

Of these three movements the second is lyrical and reflective, and the last frequently gay and uninhibited. In the first is commonly displayed the ratiocinative processes by which music can claim a place in the environment of logic. This generalization, for the moment, is a reasonable guide to the uninitiate as to what he may expect, within the field of late eighteenth- and nineteenth-century concerto. During that period structural integrity in music was as highly regarded as in architecture. Proportion qualifies classical thought and proportion is the qualification of classical music. Mozart and Haydn, as spokesmen for an era of music, show in their works why that era is known as 'classical'.

Neither music nor architecture, however, is rigid in classification and the 'norm' exists, absolutely, only in theory. Preconceived notions must be introduced only relatively. Thus while a concerto may be thought to be a musical work in three movements for a solo instrument in conjunction with orchestra there will be found many examples which do not conform to this definition. After all the word should warn us—*concerto*, 'playing together'.

⁋ DIVERSITY · In the early eighteenth century the *concerto grosso* was the centre of orchestral activity. The *concerti grossi* of Corelli or Handel comprised anything up to six movements and the contrast was not between one solo instrument and the orchestra, but between a small group of instruments (two violins and violoncello) and the main body. The American composer Robert Russell Bennett has written a startling counterpart to this arrangement. In a work entitled *Concerto grosso* his smaller body—the *concertino*, or 'little concerto' of the eighteenth century—is a dance band. He writes five movements: präludium, dialogue (ingénue and juvenile), theme song, comedy scene and blackout, and martial finale with flags. Whether this music is good or bad is beside the point. What Russell attempts is to bring music within the common experience, as indeed Handel, by *his* use of contemporary dance patterns, did. Another work in this genre is Rolf Liebermann's *Concerto for Jazz-Band and Symphony Orchestra*, which brought to the Royal Festival Hall plebeian boogie-woogie, its legitimacy guaranteed by Sir Eugene Goossens. In a more earnest way Vaughan Williams has contrived a *concerto grosso* in which groups of amateurs (some of whom need go no further than the open strings) may combine with professionals. Ernest Chausson has a one-movement *Poème* for violin and orchestra at one end of the concerto scale and a four-movement sextet for violin, piano, and string quartet (which he entitled *Concerto*) at the other.

Works which are, in effect, of the order of concerto will be discovered under many different heads: certain variations, rhapsodies, tone poems, symphonic poems all qualifying for consideration. In all cases, however, there is an incentive to present, more or less dramatically, a contrast in tone values.

Concerto, then, is not a term of strictly limited significance, but is used as a statement of a composer's general intention. In working out his project the composer is aware of precedents, the application of which has formed a general tradition; but, just as no two portraits are the same although belonging to the same *genre*, each concerto is a separate experience. This becomes more apparent when the main tradition, to which we may now turn, is known at least in outline.

III. The Concerto Tradition

IT TAKES THREE to make a musical work: listener, performer, and composer. Each has his responsibility towards the art of music, and towards his partners; so that, in the end, each community has the type of music it deserves. The history of music, therefore, is an aspect of social history; and to understand why certain instruments and modes of expression are in vogue during particular periods, because of special circumstances, may well enrich our general understanding.

❡ HUMANISM AND MUSIC · Instrumental music came into its own during the sixteenth and seventeenth centuries; when the humanist ideals of the Renaissance stimulated interest in music for its own sake, and a scientific attitude prompted fresh consideration of acoustic and musical theory. In both respects the results of enquiry and experiment were fruitful. It is not surprising that instrumental music began its growth towards independence in Italy, where in every phase of architecture, painting, literature, and philosophy the spirit of the Renaissance was manifest. The course of the arts was charted by the aristocratic rulers of the separate states into which Italy was then divided, and each vied with the others in advertising his virtues as a humanist. As a guide-book to Italy of the seventeenth century none is more lively than that part of Evelyn's *Diary* which records his Italian tour of 1646.

⁋ ITALY · Evelyn visited the opera, heard some church music made in the new manner—with recitative and aria—and noted the enthusiasm of the Italian peasantry for music. What impressed him in all he heard was the delight of the Italians in melody and beauty of sound. Evelyn was not idle regarding his own musical education. He learned to play the lute, persuading his tutor's elegant daughter (who played nine instruments) to present him with specimens of her own composition. In Venice he admired the admirable singer 'Anna Renche, whom we invited to a fish dinner after foure daies in Lent'. Characteristic of the dilettante, he noted the beauty of the women singers he heard, but nothing of the style of the music; it seemed, however, that whatever he heard, whether by voice or instrument, was expressive. Expression, indeed, was something of an end in itself.

Throughout the second half of the seventeenth century two names were prominent in Italy; those of Amati and Stradivari. They, the great violin makers of their age, were architects of the orchestral music of the future, for their labours showed indisputably the emotional and virtuoso possibilities of the violin family, as opposed to that of the viols. The viols, of mediaeval origin, were to be found in theatre and church orchestras until the beginning of the eighteenth century. But obsolescence is a gradual process and what is thought by the *avant-garde* to be behind the times shows great reluctance to recognize the case.

⁋ SONATA · Throughout fashionable opera and cantata melody reigned supreme and the violinist, able to display talent for brilliance in one way, saw to it that his art also supplied the current need for finely wrought melodic patterns. In the seventeenth century we see the birth of the solo sonata. There were two types of sonata, the one called *sonata da chiesa* (church sonata), the other *sonata da camera*. The first type represented music played in church as required, and as a change from organ interludes; the second was for secular usage. The *sonata da chiesa* was on the side of solemnity and in fugal structure (that is, the imitative and contrapuntal method familiarized in the 'old' manner of the great sixteenth-century church composers) recalled the practice of choral music. The secular sonata included dance movements. In general, sonatas of either sort included four movements, alternately slow and fast, and all but the third normally in the same key.

❡ ARCANGELO CORELLI (1653–1713) · The efforts of many Italian composers in this direction are summarized in the works of Arcangelo Corelli. Correlli, after travelling widely as a violinist, settled in Rome in 1685, and quickly established himself as performer and composer. Of engaging appearance and charming courtesy, a lover of arts other than his own and a discriminating collector of paintings, Corelli was fortunate in gaining for himself the interest and friendship of the Cardinal Ottoboni. Ottoboni was a characteristic Renaissance prelate. Nepotically raised to the purple, he was given profitable sinecures by his uncle, the Pope, so that he was able to indulge his love of poetry, music, and philosophy to the full. He installed Corelli in his palace and ordered concerts to be given each Wednesday. Since, in addition to the music of Corelli, there were also free drinks the concerts were well attended.

❡ CORELLI AND CONCERTO · For his Wednesday evenings Corelli provided sonatas and concertos. The concertos resembled the sonatas in structure, and again some had been designed for ecclesiastical use. The most notable of these latter is the so-called 'Christmas' concerto, which, in imitating the traditional Christmas Eve music of the Roman bagpipes, was deliberately picturesque. In case the respect paid to Corelli by historians tempts the listener, who feels himself odd man out, to condemn his own apparent tastelessness it may be well to observe that there were those among his contemporaries who found the music of Corelli dull. One such was the King of Naples, who once walked out in the middle of a slow movement as a protest.

Corelli, however, laid the foundations of orchestral style. He was a patient, but masterful, orchestral director and inculcated in his players discipline both in bowing and in rhythm. (This he

did by example, for he directed the ensemble from his first violin
desk.) He made the string orchestra a balanced family independent of the theatre and church bands of his day. His concertos
were laid out for a large group—the *concerto grosso*, and a small
contrasted group—the *concertino*, consisting of two violins and
cello. The viola was avoided because viola playing was un-
fashionable, and the worst violinists were put to it in the hope
that their errors might be less patent.

❡ INFLUENCE OF CORELLI · Foreign musicians in Rome made
a point of negotiating invitations to Ottoboni's Wednesday
evenings, and invariably they went home and composed series of
concertos or sonatas, cast in the new fashion of Rome. Corelli's
music, wrote Sir John Hawkins, 'was heard with delight in
churches, in theatres, at public solemnities and festivities in all
the cities of Europe for near forty years. Men remembered, and
would refer to passages [of his] as to a classic author.' It is as to
a classic author that we may refer to Corelli to-day.

Among those who followed in the wake of Corelli were
Muffat the German; Geminiani, who migrated to England;
Locatelli, whose main work was in Holland; and Handel, who
was a guest at the Ottoboni palace in 1708. Handel's *concerti
grossi*, more man-of-the-world than those of Corelli, are among
his noblest works.

The fine balance between the contrasted groups of the *concerto
grosso* (recalling the contrast to be obtained between the different
manuals of organ or harpsichord) could easily be upset if the
personality of one instrument of the *concertino* obtruded. But it
was inevitable that, sooner or later, the substitution of one instrument for three should be made. (The *concertino* is a body in which
the separate members should be co-equal in importance, but the
listener tending now, as in the seventeenth century, to concentrate his interest in the top part, may overlook the fact.)

❡ SOLO CONCERTO · So we come to Torelli, who published in
1708 a set of concertos, in one of which the *concertino* was reduced
to a single violin. It was, however, Vivaldi who commanded
universal attention by reason of his variety of tone colour, his
lithe brilliance, and his treatment of the solo concerto.

He belonged to Venice where there was a rich tradition of orchestral music in the cathedral of St Mark, in which Vivaldi —his father being a member of the orchestra—was brought up.

For a long time Venice had been remarkable for the adventurous quality of its music. Such forward-looking composers as Zarlino, the Gabrielis, and Claudio Monteverdi were intimately associated with the musical life of the Republic. Monteverdi's works, especially the operas and the *Vespers*, illustrate even today the fascination which his works must have exercised on account of their splendid diffusion of instrumental tone colour.

¶ ANTONIO VIVALDI (*c.* 1675–1741) · Vivaldi was a pupil of Giovanni Legrenzi, an industrious composer but principally to be remembered on account of his reform of the orchestra at St Mark's. Under his jurisdiction the cathedral music included 8 violins, 11 violette, 2 viole de braccia, 2 viola da gamba, 1 violone, 4 theorbos, 2 cornets, 1 bassoon, and 3 trombones. In addition to the music of the great church there was that to be heard in the city's sixteen theatres. It was for the provision of singers for these theatres that conservatories were inaugurated at the Charity Schools. Vivaldi directed the music at the most notable of these institutions, the *Ospedale della Pieta*. Here, with choir and orchestra and the task of instructing young performers, he had every incentive to experiment as a composer.

Vivaldi, noting the fashion and general style of the *concerto grosso*, inflected it with a Venetian accent. Corelli's dignity and fine sculpting is wholly admirable. Vivaldi's brilliance of outline and wealth of colouring is exciting. Vivaldi found some relationship between musical sounds and visual or literary images, and his concertos include a number which bear evocative titles. Of these the most familiar are the four for solo violin and strings entitled *The Four Seasons*. Whether these appear as illustrative or not makes no odds: the possiblity is that they might have inspired Vivaldi to consider all sorts of instrumental combinations. A 'Funeral Concerto', for instance, includes a chorus of various members of the oboe group. A violinist himself, Vivaldi composed many concertos for that instrument; but he also explored

c

the potential of other instruments—his vast output contains concertos for flute, bassoon, oboe, and viola d'amore. It is only a minority of Vivaldi's works that have yet been revised and reissued.

❰ JOHN SEBASTIAN BACH (1685–1750) · As was the case with Corelli, Vivaldi, evidently aided by some flair for public relations, drew attention to his works by the excellence of his performances, and their influence went far afield. So it was that John Sebastian Bach, in search of music for the court at Cöthen or the Musical Society at the University in Leipzig, came across the works of Vivaldi, and, appreciating their vitality, transcribed a number of them for his own use.

❰ GEORGE FRIDERIC HANDEL (1685–1759) · While Bach was playing his concertos in Leipzig Handel was equally busy in London. At one extreme there were ceremonial concerto-type works such as the *Water Music* and the *Music for the Royal Fireworks*, at the other delicate works for organ, a chamber organ without pedals, and orchestra. These latter Handel himself used to play in the intervals of his oratorios, and it may be felt that in the organ concertos there is sometimes a certain appositeness to particular oratorios. Some contemporary organists have the temerity to use less than all of their stops all the time. Handel's concertos under such conditions are a revelation.

While four was a not unusual number of movements for a *concerto grosso* there was considerable freedom. Presumably it depended on how much music audiences were willing to stand. The first Brandenburg concerto, after three movements more or less according to schedule, runs off into a sequence of dances. If all are played as is proposed the listener may well experience musical indigestion. But the baroque period was nothing if not generous.

❰ THE 'BAROQUE' · Take the case, for instance, of Carbonelli's benefit in 1722, Carbonelli being a celebrated violinist in London. A concerto for two trumpets by Grano, a *concerto grosso* by Albinoni, a concerto by Carbonelli himself, a concerto for two oboes and two flutes by Dieupart, a concerto on the bass-viol by Pippo[1],

---

[1] Filippo Amadei, known in England as 'Signor Pippo'.

the eighth—the 'Christmas'—concerto by Corelli. And so on, until the affair ended with another performance by the two trumpets.

A creative artist, or a greatly productive period, leaves a mass of untidiness, which becomes the despair of the next generation and the delight of subsequent scholars. The concertos of the baroque period have suffered at the hands of posterity. First they were held up as undernourished ancestors of classical concerto. Next, in comparison with romantic concertos, they tended to be neglected as drily academic. Now they return to favour, but rather often under the zealous guardianship of pedants. The music of Corelli, Vivaldi, Bach, and Handel in this sphere stands gravely eloquent of a great age, and any performance (whether 'correct' or 'incorrect') which fails to release eloquence is failure.

⁋ RITORNELLO · It has been seen that indirectly the traditions of church and theatre contributed to the modes of expression employed. There was, as well, the influence of the dance, for bourrée and jig, minuet and polacca have their place in the concerto. The prevailing formal characteristic, however, to be noted in the main movements is that known as *ritornello*, yet another example of the dominance of Italy. In any one of the main movements of the Brandenburg concertos it will be noticed that the opening phrase is repeated a number of times in the course of the movement, in different keys. This method, to be seen also in vocal and choral music (especially, for instance, in the great choruses of Bach's major choral works, which in themselves are of a *concertante* nature), imposes a structural unity. The *ritornello* principle, as demonstrated by Arthur Hutchings in his *Companion to Mozart's Piano Concertos*, prevails also in the first movements of Mozart's concertos.

But as between the concertos of Handel and Bach, and those of Mozart, there is a world of difference.

⁋ ENLIGHTENMENT · The listener may make his own distinctions. If he arrives at the conclusion that in Mozart there is more charm, more gaiety, more 'emotion', more colour, more melody, less untidiness, less untowardness of instrumentation, less complexity of texture, he will have gratified the shades of Carl Philipp

Emanuel and John Christian Bach, the two sons of John Sebastian, who were among pioneers of the idea of *Aufklärung*, or 'enlightment', in music. He will, incidentally, have misunderstood the quality of the senior Bach—but that one comes back to.

There comes a point when any idea, or set of ideas, appears irrevocably old-fashioned, out-of-date. Hardly was the ink dry on J. S. Bach's *Art of Fugue* or Handel's *Jephtha* before the bright young men declared that music's golden future lay in propositions less associated with scholarship on the one hand, and the Bible on the other. Suavity in melody, easy elegance in harmony, formal neatness, precision in orchestral lay-out, expressiveness, but not too much passion: these were the qualities to be imparted to music just as they had been to architecture, painting, and interior decoration. The influence of the artists employed by Louis XIV and XV, and approved by the Mesdames Pompadour and du Barry, spread across the whole of Europe and the style known as rococo became commonplace. Music can never quite be equated with stylistic conventions in other arts because of an inevitably greater strain of emotional intensity. But between them the immediate predecessors of Mozart did their best to achieve rococo standards. Music which for long had owed allegiance to the Church in greater or lesser degree was now dominated by the atmosphere of the salon.

⁋ NEW STYLE · C. P. E. Bach, employed at Potsdam by Frederick the Great, was conscious of the aspirations of his time and sought to fulfil them, but with dignity and sincerity. He it was who, taking the patterns of Italian keyboard works and giving to them proportion and dignity, formulated the general shape of the classical sonata. Both Haydn and Mozart acknowledged their debt to him. As for John Christian his volatile genius led him away from Germany; first to Milan, and then to London, where he settled as composer and impresario. John Christian's symphonies, among the earliest of their kind, are impregnate with a sweet reasonableness and may be commended as agreeable diversions. In these symphonies, as in his concertos, and other contemporary works, it is noticeable that the design depends on the balance not only of melodies but also of keys, which in 'classical' music are arranged in sequences that always appear as logical.

A musical tour of Europe in the mid-eighteenth century would have passed through Mannheim where, under the tutelage of Johann Stamitz, the orchestra was one of the wonders of the age. Brilliant, colourful, disciplined, the band, comprising strings, flutes, oboes, clarinets, bassoons, horns, and trumpets, set a standard which became an ideal for orchestras everywhere. Players trained at Mannheim went to Paris, to Munich, and London; music composed by pupils of the elder Stamitz was printed in Paris, Amsterdam, and London.

As a boy Mozart heard the music of John Christian Bach in London and it made a great impression on him. His earliest symphonies and concertos, indeed, were deliberately based on models by Bach. As a touring child prodigy Mozart took with him such works as exemplified his own talents as player and composer and which could be readily performed by the instrumental resources of any small court. Hence the *Tre Sonate del Sgr. Giovanni Bach ridotte in Concerto del Sgr. Amadeo Wolfgang Mozart* (K. 107) which required only two violins and bass for the *tutti* passages. These three concertos were probably composed for harpsichord; but the harpsichord was not a favourite instrument of Mozart.

❡ THE PIANOFORTE · In the early years of the eighteenth century the instrument makers Cristofori, Schröter, and Silbermann had developed the pianoforte and specimens of their manufacture were to be found in the possession of many keen amateurs. The most notable of these was Frederick the Great, who proudly showed his Silbermann instruments to J. S. Bach when he visited Potsdam. But composers in general had shown little enthusiasm. It was Mozart who raised the pianoforte—and the pianist—to its position of eminence. He was brought up to the instruments of Späth of Regensburg, but came to prefer those of Stein of Augsburg. These he commended on account of their evenness of tone.

Mozart, the student of Wagenseil, Raupach, Honauer, Schobert, Eckhardt, and the Bachs (all 'popular' composers of Mozart's youth), and appreciating the potentialities of the pianoforte, created some thirty works of the concerto-type for this instrument alone. His keen ear, surely the keenest in musical history, also observed the qualities of other instruments whose importance was slight, and there are concertos for violin, bassoon, oboe, flute, flute and harp, horn and clarinet, as well as a *sinfonia concertante* for violin and viola.

In general Mozart's concertos had three movements. The first was within the outlines of sonata form (see p. 48), the second slow and with much embellishment in the solo part, the third in the manner of a *rondo*. But this was not always the case, for airs with variations—always a joy to the listener—sometimes took the place of second or third movements. The qualities which the listener may well descry in these works have already been indicated. What the listener will not discover will be any hints as to Mozart's personal affairs, or emotional problems. His music stands in sublime independence and, contrived almost without exception for the requirements of his age, exemplifies the attitude of the composer-craftsman. The eighteenth-century artist made what he was asked to make, and was often hard put to it to keep up with the demand.

❡ ROMANTICISM · In the nineteenth century it was different. The composer, no longer content with the subordinate status occupied by his predecessors, began to take himself seriously. One result of Rousseauism and *The Rights of Man*, and the intolerable manners of the *ancien régime*, was that everyone began to take himself seriously. Classical music may have had a 'soul': if so no-one said so. Nineteenth-century music at its worst is exceedingly soulful.

Keats, who seems to have used the word soul as frequently as any poet, recognized the way to decadence in the Preface to *Endymion*:

'The imagination of a boy is healthy, and the mature imagination of a man healthy; but there is a space of life between, in which the soul is in a ferment, the character undecided, the way of life uncertain, the ambition thick-sighted: thence proceeds mawkishness.' Let that be the criterion in considering the Romantic movement.

Beethoven, it must at once be said, had 'the mature imagination of a man': nonetheless he saw himself as the great preceptor
and his music was often intended to admonish, to instruct. Music
to Beethoven was no casual matter, fit for the delectation of idle
wits, but a revelation. To the Archduke Rudolph he expressed
himself explicitly: 'Liberty and progress are the goals of art just
as of life in general'. Once Beethoven and Goethe were at Töplitz,
and during a walk they met the Imperial family. Goethe stood
aside. Not so Beethoven. He went straight on, through the con-
course of flabbergasted courtiers and affronted princelings. 'Kings
and princes', he wrote, 'can easily make professors and privy
councillors; they can bestow titles and decorations, but they
cannot make great men, or minds which rise above the base tur-
moil of this world—and when two men are together such as
Goethe and myself these fine gentlemen must be made conscious
of the difference between ourselves and them.'

The whole of this, and more, is within the authority of
Beethoven's concertos. In few other works is there a more comprehensive survey of thought and emotion set in purely musical
terms. The outstanding feature of Beethoven's concertos is their
dramatic content. The orchestra, now many-coloured, is more
insistent than in the eighteenth-century tradition, while the
soloist is no longer confined in scope. The first movement of the
third concerto, the third movement of the fourth concerto, and
the whole of the fifth concerto for piano, and the violin concerto
display Beethoven's genius at its greatest: the dramatic and the
lyric, the tragic and the comic lie within the immense ranges of
rhythm and colour (all attributed to their ideal mediums) which
Beethoven cultivated within the ideals of nascent Romanticism.

⁋ NINETEENTH-CENTURY STREAM-LINING · Beethoven, being
both classic and romantic as, of course, is every great artist,
looked backwards and forwards. In a lesser degree so did Mendelssohn, whose violin concerto is a landmark in concerto history.

Form is never static and, as has been suggested, the normal
never really exists—except as a textbook abstraction. But conventions appear in music and remain for a time. When conventions are dispersed the composer is inevitably regarded as pro-

gressive. (Such a composer may be—but it should never be forgotten that it is the inner quality of art which matters and not the form in which this is presented.) In his fourth piano concerto Beethoven commences at once with the piano. Now this was unusual, but the reflective listener will conclude that this is the proper opening for this particular concerto. In both the fourth and fifth concertos the last two movements are interlinked. Mendelssohn went further in the direction of unification and stream-lining, for in his violin concerto there is no break between first and second movement, and virtually none between the second and third. It will be noticed that Mendelssohn also dispenses with preliminaries in this concerto, by introducing his soloist at once—without orchestral preamble—and the *cadenza* of the first movement is written in as an integral part of the whole.

Mendelssohn had a distaste for the growing school of mere virtuosi. Pianists with technical agility and unmusical minds are a menace at all times. At the beginning of the nineteenth century, when the piano was a new instrument, there were many of them. Reicha, Neukomm, Kalkbrenner, Herz, as well as the more musical Hummel and Moscheles, poured out endless fantasias and concertos in which showmanship was all. Mendelssohn, a stern disciplinarian in regard to taste, took a poor view of concert-goers who esteemed the inanities of the day and forgot the past glories of Mozart and Haydn, Bach and Handel.

❡ SPIRIT OF THE AGE · But the spirit of an age is irresistible. That of the nineteenth century was far-ranging and ambitious. That the arts should be the concern of the many rather than of the few is an ideal often voiced at the present time; but that this is so is due to the various ways in which artists of the Romantic era explored the meaning of the revolutionary catch-phrase: *freedom, equality, fraternity*.

Freedom suggested that music need not any longer be merely musical. And so we came to the incorporation within such 'abstract' forms as symphony and concerto of literary and pictorial references.

Berlioz acknowledges his literary intent openly, and especially in the *Fantastic Symphony*. Weber (whose overtures are exquisitely evocative) does not do this in respect of his *Concertstück in F minor*, but he did outline a programme for the work to Julius Benedict, his pupil. It represents a heroic tale of the Crusades— a fashionable study for Romantic artists of all denominations. It is, I think, an illusion that a story enables one to listen more appreciatively. The *Concertstück* is a case in point. Not one listener in a hundred is even aware of the basic narrative but the general appreciation of a masterly concerto is in no way lessened. In Liszt's *Todtentanz*, on the other hand, the music (for piano and orchestra) is much less than significant when its origin in the frescoes of Orcagna in the Campo Santo at Pisa is not known. This macabre essay—linked with Berlioz's *Symphonie fantastique*, Rachmaninov's *Rhapsody on a theme of Paganini*, and Vaughan Williams's *Job*—in variation form is grotesquely illustrative. It was composed in 1849 but not played (for no-one liked it) until thirty years later, when Siloti of St Petersburg performed it in Brussels.

The tone-poem-cum-concerto has never quite lost its attraction for composers. Joachim and Manuel da Falla struck out nationalistically in the *Hungarian Concerto* and *Nights in the Gardens of Spain*. Strauss in *Don Quixote* pictured the adventures (some of them) of Don Quixote and Sancho Panza by means of solo cello and viola. Bloch's *Schelomo* (the Hebrew name for Solomon) is a rhapsody for cello and orchestra and an attempt at musical characterization. In Arthur Cohn's flute concerto an Hebraic influence is admitted into the section entitled *Kaddish* (i.e. 'Blessing', a liturgical term). Hindemith's *Der Schwanendreher*, for viola and orchestra, is a concerto based on folk melodies. In the work there is something of practically everything, for fugue and variation are the substance of the last two movements. Poulenc in his *Concert Champêtre* brings back to the modern concert room the harpsichord: at the same time he attempts deliberately to capture the spirit and style of the harpsichordists of the days of Louis XIV and Louis XV.

These, and many similar works, are, however, the entrances to *culs-de-sac*. 'Descriptive music' is immediately attractive, perhaps: but when the novelty has subsided the thought persists,

'So what?' How much further forward are we by knowing that music is like something?

❡ THE MAIN STREAM · The side track has taken us far away from the mainstream of concerto, which is independent of factitious illustration. After Beethoven there are, notably, Schumann, Brahms, Grieg, Tchaikovsky, Dvořák, Elgar, Sibelius, Bartók, Berg, Walton, as will be seen, with some considerable claim to membership of the classical order.

It is possible to establish connections between the music of these composers and the Haydn, Mozart, Beethoven triumvirate; but there is a different conception, in general, of the role of the soloist. He, or she, is patently one of outstanding technical capacity. The concerto of the nineteenth century was created for the virtuoso.

❡ VIRTUOSO · The prototype of the virtuoso was, of course, Paganini, whose extraordinary talents and garish personality created a legend.

As Paganini demonstrated the complete range of violin technique so Liszt (whose private affairs were hardly less bizarre than Paganini's, and whose performance was hardly less magical) showed the public properties of the pianoforte. Both Paganini and Liszt were not only performers but also composers, and so too were other conspicuous featurers of the nineteenth-century concerto; among them Vieuxtemps and Ysaÿe, Anton Rubinstein and Paderewski. In more recent times, however, the art of performing has become separate from that of composing and the results have not always been satisfactory. This has been the case not so much in relation to contemporary music, where skill in unfamiliar instruments has led to some welcome additions to the repertoire, but in regard to that of the classical tradition. However it seems to be quite frequently recognized that X's Mozart and Y's Beethoven have nothing to commend them over Mozart's Mozart and Beethoven's Beethoven.

The concerto of the eighteenth century was designed for an intimate atmosphere in which extreme dramatic emphasis was out of place, and in which the performer was expected to subordinate his mechanical skill to the pattern of the music. The discipline of classical music is strict, and uncongenial to the mere virtuoso; but in that its values represent an ideal for those who suspect the flamboyancies of a brasher age it is to classical music that we turn for reassurance. Thus we may now examine certain notable examples of the classical concerto in greater detail.

IV. The Classical Manner

¶ WOLFGANG AMADEUS MOZART (1756–1791) · The difficulty about Mozart, so far as the general listener is concerned, is his prolificacy. With the exception of Schubert (who, however, composed many fewer large-scale works) it is doubtful whether any other composer crowded so much into so short a time. In the face of a mass of operas, symphonies, concertos, sonatas, chamber music, liturgical music, the amateur of music may well feel perplexed. However, the man of culture is not he who appears to know everything, but he who, knowing what there is to be known about, is intimately aware of a selection of what used to be called 'elegant extracts', while generally informed as to their provenance. There will be none, counting the music to be contained in an anthology of this nature, who will not list half-a-dozen full-scale works of Mozart. Here, we may feel, is cool and reasonable music which, while infinitely varied, upholds the standards without which music could not survive. For, of all music, Mozart's is the most purely musical; and, therefore, the most classical.

The immediately apparent quality of Mozart is fluency. But to this he added a studiousness that may often be overlooked. An interest in music other than his own made him alive to new modes of expression and these, often imperceptibly grafted on to his own style, made it that no two works were quite alike. But a general conformity in late eighteenth-century style enables one to move at ease among the masterpieces of the period, to feel some immediate sympathy with them, and to appreciate their intention.

VIOLIN CONCERTOS · Masterpieces, of course, are sometimes small works—and so we may well arrive at the five violin concertos which Mozart, then nineteen years of age, composed for the Archbishop of Salzburg in 1775. These were works of supererogation. Mozart was not expected to play the violin at court (in fact his father had expressly laid it down that he should not), but in these works he did; presumably to stimulate the Archbishop's interest and generosity. Mozart should have known better; Hieronymus von Colloredo was deficient in both respects.

Style, it is often said, consists of the right words in the right order. In his violin concertos Mozart shows how effortlessly he arrived at a precise style. But style alone is insufficient to captivate and so it is that we become aware of Mozart's wit. The wit in these concertos is that of a young man, disarmingly impertinent; but it is balanced by a capacity for tranquillity which is more remarkable. So, while the concertos echo the familiar models of Tartini and Locatelli, Pugnani and Boccherini, there is evident the impress of an independent personality.

The second movement of the third concerto may be instanced. Here is the utmost simplicity. The score has strings, 2 flutes, and 2 horns, in addition to the solo instrument. The strings are muted. The flutes replace the oboes which are elsewhere employed. The horns are restricted to the essential notes of the tonic and dominant chords. The melody, immediately given in the orchestral *ritornello*, is based on an arpeggio figure: a commonplace. The accompaniment figure, of undulating triplets, is as apparently negligible as in many works of the same period.

But Mozart integrates these separate elements and imposes an ineluctable unity. There is unity of form, but there is more; there is unity of idea. This is accomplished by the allusions of the soloist to the observations of the rest of the orchestra; but also by the spaciousness of the whole design. The solo violin arches over the whole movement. There may be noted the points of entry and of departure.

In October 1777 Mozart was in Augsburg and one evening a concert was arranged at the Convent of the Holy Cross. It was an engaging company that settled down to a Mozart evening, and one of the works that gained great applause was the fourth violin concerto. 'It went', wrote Wolfgang to his father, 'like oil.' Nor was it an unprofitable evening, for he cleared seventy florins after his expenses were paid.

The first movement—*allegro*—is full of ebullience. The second is an extended song for the soloist. The third is a rondo. A rondo is a movement in which (as in the literary *rondeau*) the one strain recurs. We may examine this example more closely, for its divisions are readily apparent to the ear. The violin announces a gay melody in 2/4 time and in the key of D major. At the fifteenth bar the rhythm is changed to 3/8, and the soloist is supported first by the violins only, then with additional notes (widely spaced) by horn and oboe. With the entry of the lower strings the section expands vivaciously. This concluded—not in the key of D but in that of A (the dominant)—the first 2/4 section re-appears. Then the second section once more. But this time the conclusion is different. The harmony is more interrogatory and the scoring clearly suggests a new departure, for the solo violin is left alone in the company of oboes and horns.

An entirely new idea is now interpolated. A melody of such innocence that the music of the kindergarten is within earshot. We may note that for periods the violinist holds a long note against this melody. Such was the quality of the popular French *musette*, which Mozart had in mind when he wrote this movement. The *musette*, which started in the key of G (the subdominant to D), veers towards A major, from which, as the dominant to D, we are returned to the two sections which have already made two appearances in the movement. The *musette* interpolation is in imitation of a similar melody which Karl von Dittersdorf, a Viennese musician who was the friend both of Mozart and Haydn, wrote in a symphony. Von Dittersdorf named his melody 'ballo Strasburghese', and so Mozart referred to his concerto as the 'Strasbourg Concerto'.

The clear divisions of the rondo in the fourth of the violin concertos gives a good idea of this form of structure. Rondos are frequent as the last movements of classical music, but seldom are they divided, as here, into such clearly defined and separate paragraphs.

The last movement of the fifth concerto is also of provocative charm. It is a minuet with all the grace that might be expected. In mid-course, however, the courtesies are extinguished by an irruption that is none the less vicious because only a handful of instruments are playing. This, indeed, is a fine example of dramatic placing. Moreover the sudden change from A major to A minor is chilling. This episode—an *alla turca* (see also the piano sonata in A major, K. 331)—was lifted from a bizarre ballet which Mozart incorporated in his Milanese opera *Lucio Silla*. After the *alla turca* the minuet resumes its course. Why did Mozart thus break the mould? From a wish to experiment? From bravado? Or from some distaste for the social conventions that the minuet represented? There is no final answer; but behind any art is the artist. Mozart had a fair contempt for the insincerities of high life, and while continually creating pearls did not forget that sometimes they would be cast before swine.

The final movements from the fourth and fifth violin concertos relatively are not 'important'; but they have such fascination that they are likely to linger in the memory. The opening movements of the concertos, without the tantalizing episodes, are of a higher unity and make their impression as a whole, as supple examples of the structural principles on which all classical music was constructed.

PIANO CONCERTOS · These principles may be examined by a more or less detailed consideration of a complete, and representative, concerto. If the reader has followed a previous suggestion and invested in the score of the A major piano concerto (K. 488) he will be able to see the ground plan.

At the outset a clear-eyed melody in A major (theme A) is announced by the violins. The accompaniment is by the rest of the string ensemble. At letter [D] of the score the piano enters alone, and delivers the same material, somewhat embellished. For the moment the soloist is left alone. At letter [H] the opening theme appears yet again, and the key is again that of A major. But the character of a theme only emerges when it is seen to stand in contrast to other themes. So we return to the orchestral opening. At letter [A] the whole orchestra is engaged in the display of material of greater solidity. This (theme B) comes to a stop at letter [B] in the key of E major, the dominant. Now a third melody, distinguished from the first and second by commencing on a weak beat and thereby gaining elasticity of movement, is given. This—theme C—expands and is coloured by bassoon and flute on either side of the violins. The orchestral introduction ends with a fourth melodic group (theme D), in which the full complement of instruments is involved, and in which the woodwind will be seen to play an important, and occasionally independent, role. Within each melodic group there is an inner organization, fragments being repeated either exactly or with such modification as will lead easily to new phrases.

We have then themes A, B, C, D. When the piano is introduced, themes A, B, and C are repeated. But the melodies are varied, being divided between the soloist and the *tutti*, who conduct a dialogue. So far as the piano is concerned the variants are devised to display what is patently a keyboard style: moreover, by economy in the orchestration the dialogue is on equal terms. But there is, throughout theme B, a changing atmosphere, so that when C arrives we are aware of a fundamental alteration. In fact the key now is not A major, but E major; and so it continues for some considerable time.

From now on the keys change rapidly while a new melodic and rhythmic figure is introduced to contrast with an already familiar phrase which is now prominently assigned to clarinets and bassoons. The piano increases in prominence until a generous flourish, based on chords which inevitably lead back to the key of A major, heralds the entire group announced first in the orchestral prelude. The repetition, however, is not quite exact: A, B, C, and then a quotation from the middle of the work which is halted by four striking chords. The cadenza follows. And finally an orchestral peroration, which, derived from D, is conclusive.

The second movement—*andante*—is less complex in structure, but more instinct with emotion. The quality now is as of a song, of which the contours have been idealized into patterns apt for the piano. The piano commences in the key of F sharp minor—the 'relative' minor key to A major, which will be seen to have the same sharps in the key signature—and is allowed eleven bars before the entry of the orchestra. When the orchestra has entered, a plangent phrase outlined by the woodwind reaches to an impassioned cadence. Here the piano overlaps to state a new sentence. This moves away from F sharp minor to a middle paragraph, largely in A major, in which the orchestral colouring is of great beauty, and great clarity, and in turn the piano adds a gentle radiance in its figuration. A final paragraph, balancing the first, and firmly situated in the key of the movement, follows. In the paragraph the *pizzicato* strings, in broken octaves, induce an ominous note: at the end the natural melancholy of the key is enhanced by the high notes of the woodwind.

There follows a rondo movement of sparkling wit. The way in which this concerto is designed demonstrates the intellectual basis of the work and shows a general method of organizing musical composition. But no composer is rule-bound and Mozart adapted the conventions of formal design to suit his imaginative ideas. So, in detail, each concerto is a special case. With the general principles (especially of key relationship) in mind, however, the listener is more qualified to perceive the felicities of detail.

The A major concerto was composed at the beginning of March, 1786. At the end of the month the concerto in C minor (K. 491) was completed. These concertos, as was the case with those belonging to each of the two previous years, were intended for performance at the winter series of subscription concerts in

D

Vienna. The patrons of these concerts did not always find Mozart easy to understand. The C minor concerto in relation to its predecessor shows why this was so. The concerto in A is within the eighteenth century and hazards no prophecies, whereas its companion, highly favoured by Beethoven, expounds a high seriousness (as Matthew Arnold would call it) that is, even now, disturbing in its implications. This is a work which asks questions rather than states propositions. The scale of the orchestral opening, the unexpected entry of the piano, the disquieting interpolation of alien keys, the largeness of the scoring all indicate a profundity of approach. This concerto, with flute, oboes, clarinets, bassoons, horns, trumpets, drums, in addition to strings, employs a larger orchestra than was customary and the design of the concerto as a whole is not unrelated to the scale of the orchestration.

In K. 488 the second movement was in the key of the relative minor. In K. 491, the whole work being in C minor, the intermediate *larghetto* is in the relative major. As befits the character of the movement the trumpets and drums are omitted. The design lies between rondo and air with variations; another instance of Mozart's unwillingness to be hide-bound. After the *larghetto* is a fine movement, consisting of eight variations with a coda, on a theme, in which the conflict of emotion is indicated in the strenuous outline. The C major concerto (K. 503), written at the end of 1786, is the last of the concertos composed for the subscribers to the winter concerts in Vienna.

FOR VARIOUS INSTRUMENTS · The decade which separated the violin concertos and the piano concertos which have been under discussion saw an amazing profusion of concertos of different types. In 1776 the concerto for three pianos was written, with the capabilities of the players in mind, for Countess Lodron and her daughters. Two years later the flute concertos were composed for the Duc de Guines, formerly French Ambassador in London, whom Mozart met in Paris. Since the Duke's daughter played the harp it is not surpising that there is one concerto for flute and harp. There followed the *sinfonia concertante*, in E flat, for violin and viola, in which the importance of the orchestral writing shows the effective influence of the Mannheim orchestra; and the

four horn concertos, which bring an open-air feeling to the salon.
MORE PIANO CONCERTOS · All the time piano concertos were
being produced. Until 1782 a number of concertos were written
for performance in Salzburg, and sometimes for the benefit of
visiting players of distinction. In the autumn of 1782 began the
great series of concertos for Vienna.

Of the concertos, and in addition to those already noted, that
in D minor (K. 466) is most likely to cross the listener's path.
Herein the first movement looks ahead to the more severe
thoughts of the C minor concerto, and of the G minor symphony
and the *Requiem Mass*. The slow movement entitled *Romanza*, is,
however, a sentimental essay which has little relation to the
surrounding movements.

The circumstances of the first performance of this concerto, as
described by Leopold Mozart, show how far from ideal conditions could be. 'We had a new and very fine concerto by Wolfgang, which the copyist was still copying when we arrived, and
the rondo of which your brother did not even have time to play
through, as he had to supervise the copying.'

In the same letter there is reference to the effect made by
Mozart's playing of a charming concerto (K. 456 in B flat) before
the Court: '. . . Your brother played a glorious concerto which he
composed for Mlle Paradis [a blind pianist] of Paris. I was sitting
only two boxes away from the very beautiful Princess of Wurtem-
berg and had the great pleasure of hearing so clearly all the interplay of the instruments that for sheer delight tears came into my
eyes. When your brother left the platform the Emperor waved
his hat and called out "Bravo, Mozart!" '

For sheer consistency there are few composers who can compare with Mozart (an eighteenth-century composer was, of course,
expected to be consistent) and the temptation to say 'Bravo,
Mozart' is at all times strong: that is if one has the courtesy to
remember Mozart, the composer, behind the present virtuoso
who lays claim not only to the first 'Bravo', but also, often, to
the last. Pianists are as thick as the autumnal leaves in Vallom-
brosa, but not many of Mozart's concertos find welcome in their
repertoires. The reason is not far to find.

CLARINET CONCERTO · Fortunately clarinettists, who are not overstocked with party pieces, are obliged to carry Mozart at the head of their list. The clarinet concerto (K. 622) is a very late work; the last concerto, indeed, that Mozart wrote. In some ways it may have some claim to consideration as the finest of all his concertos. The solo part, without ostentation at any point, is a comprehensive account of the soul of the instrument. Beyond this, one may feel, there is little more that can be said to add to our knowledge of the character and capacity of the clarinet.

It is, perhaps, the slow movement that will remain longest in mind, with a broad melodic sweep that is both simple and profound. Herein is the full characterization, for this melody means much less when transferred to another medium. The continual contrast between the high and low registers of the instrument—see, especially, the slow movement—distinguishes the clarinet, but the faculty for mastering these extremes was new in Mozart's day. Had it not been for his friend Anton Stadler, who also came from Salzburg to Vienna, Mozart would not have been able to exploit the instrument (whose tonal properties he had marked at Mannheim) as he did. Stadler extended the tone of the clarinet downward, thus incorporating some of the richness which belonged to the basset-horn, soon to become obsolete. It is clear, too, that Stadler's tone was mellow and round, for this was the German-Austrian tradition as opposed to the French.

Stadler's playing stimulated not only the clarinet concerto, but also the trio for piano, clarinet, and viola (K. 498), and the clarinet quintet (K. 581). The concerto is, as it were, the summary of all that Mozart had previously thought in terms of the clarinet. Throughout, its voice is enriched by the varied tones of the *tutti*—strings, flute, horns, and bassoons—and the whole conception is a masterpiece of integration. 'One almost has the impression', writes Dr Einstein, 'that Mozart felt impelled to express again, in greater and dramatically animated form, what he had already expressed in more lyric form in the domain of chamber music.'

The last movement of the clarinet concerto was scored a week after the first performance of *Die Zauberflöte*. This took place after Mozart's return from Prague, from directing *La clemenza di Tito* (commissioned for the coronation of Leopold II as King of Bohemia). Stadler had gone to Prague with Mozart and his performances of the *obbligati* in two arias of the opera were winning mighty applause. So Mozart, heartened by his friend's success, got down to his finale. He wrote to his wife at Baden: 'Immediately after your departure I played two games of billiards with Herr von Mozart, the fellow who wrote the opera which is running at Schickaneder's theatre; then I sold my nag for fourteen ducats; then I told Joseph to get Primus to fetch me some black coffee, with which I smoked a splendid pipe of tobacco; and then I orchestrated almost the whole of Stadler's rondo.'

It is salutary sometimes to remember that Mozart was very down-to-earth: which is as it should be, for in its origins art is human, and the artist and his audience start from points of common interest. The artist, however, ranges further afield and discovers beyond the common the uncommon.

⁅ JOSEPH HAYDN (1732–1809) · There is the case of Haydn. Haydn, who was of age before Mozart was born and yet lived on for eighteen years after Mozart's death, was a commonplace person: kind, scrupulous, a little tetchy as he grew older, always waggish, with no ambitions in the world beyond his competence as a court servant, he was of the type that has for its testimonial 'he is a good mixer'. He was the father of the classical symphony and of the string quartet, the composer of some of the best sonatas of his age and of two great oratorios. His concertos hold no comparable position either to the quartets or to the symphonies; but two of them communicate so admirably the composer's everyday geniality that they answer the low esteem in which they are academically held by remaining permanently in the common ear.

TRUMPET CONCERTO · The trumpet concerto is just the sort of work that the trumpeter enjoys. As a community brass players preserve some of the humours which one learns to associate with Haydn. Thus, in general, they go through the trumpet concerto with a clear conviction that their job is to play what the composer wrote (even if his high notes demand some considerable skill)—

and no frills. Not long ago I played this work with George Eskdale, who shows his affection for the work by a completely satisfying and musicianly approach. That, he implies, at the end, is that; and walks off.

Haydn wrote this concerto for a Viennese court trumpeter, Anton Weidinger, who was using a keyed trumpet (keys were used before valves to fill up the gaps between the 'open' notes of the natural trumpet). Haydn's concerto was written in 1796. Seven years later Hummel also wrote a concerto for Weidinger.

The trumpet concerto has infectious tunes in the outside movements, and more than a touch of pathos in the *adagio*. In the cello concerto there is again the same infectious quality. The first tune of the first movement and the principal theme of the rondo are irresistible. There is about this music a domestic quality, for most of Haydn's concertos were composed at Esterház where he was so happily employed with the Prince's household for thirty years. They are unambitious works but of clubbable quality. Haydn's orchestra at Esterház comprised 11 violins, 2 violas, 2 cellos, 2 basses, 2 oboes, 2 bassoons, and 2 horns; and a much larger ensemble—such as demanded by Gevaert's re-orchestration of the cello concerto—destroys the intimacy of the music.

❡ INTERPRETATION · This brings us aptly to a point which is bound to come somewhere sooner or later. To what extent should we perform works as they were originally performed? At the outset we should generally disapprove of accretions. Laboured cadenzas are the obviously objectionable additions to the late eighteenth-century style. Mozart left some cadenzas of his own (catalogued as K. 624), which are but brief and slender embellishments. These should serve as models. Of cadenzas supplied by others for Mozart the most interesting are those which Beethoven composed for the concerto that he especially admired, that in D minor.

The contemporary concert orchestra is, of course, the child of the nineteenth century and usually far too large for dealing with Mozartian delicacies. Therefore a relatively small combination is required, against which the soloist does not have to struggle for survival. The modern grand pianoforte can, obviously, compete not unsuccessfully with a large orchestra, but only by sacrificing the virtues for which we esteem Mozart. Lucidity and limpidity are the qualities to be looked for, and the gift of understatement. Therefore, excesses of *rubato*, of over-dramatic treatment of dynamics, of pedalling are all out of place.

It is, on the other hand, impossible to put the clock back. We cannot reproduce the exact conditions of the eighteenth (or any other) century. To supply a grand pianoforte of *circa* 1800, wind instruments with the primitive key systems then employed, valve-less horns and trumpets would be manifestly absurd: even if it were possible. We can, however, by bearing in mind what performances of a particular date would not have included modify our views on 'interpretation' so that balance and proportion are maintained.

In the first half of the nineteenth century the makers of pianos were legion, and there was hardly one who had not some invention of his own to patent. It was the introduction of metal bracing —which allowed a larger keyboard, of a 'repetition action'— by which 'touch' was improved, and of pedals, which gave the piano characteristics of which composers were quick to avail themselves. All these major developments took place within the lifetime of Beethoven and are reflected in the whole of Beethoven's keyboard writing. His pianoforte concertos, then, take us into a new field.

❴ LUDWIG VAN BEETHOVEN (1770–1827)

PIANO CONCERTOS · There are five pianoforte concertos by Beethoven: in C major (No. 1), composed in 1797; in B flat (No. 2), composed in 1795, but revised in 1798; in C minor (No. 3), composed in 1800; in G major (No. 4), composed in 1805; and in E flat (No. 5, known, without warrant, as 'The Emperor'), composed in 1809.

The Bohemian composer and pianist Jan Tomašek heard Beethoven play the first two concertos in Vienna in 1798. He found the new music, to say the least of it, surprising: 'I admired his powerful and brilliant playing, but his frequent daring deviations from one motiv to another, whereby the organic connection, the gradual development of idea was put aside, did not escape me. Evils of this nature frequently weaken his greatest compositions, those which sprang from a too exuberant conception.'

Tomašek did not realize that Beethoven's *purpose*, in composing music, was radically different from Mozart's. Shock tactics were part of the spirit of Romantic expression: they were also part of Beethoven's personality. Naturally composers learn from their predecessors and that Beethoven was a student of Mozart and Haydn, as well as of Hummel and other writers of piano music, is apparent.

But it is at once clear from the opening of the orchestral *ritornello* of the first piano concerto that, even if the design of the work is similar to that of previous concertos, there is a startling novelty in mood. The *pianissimo* at the outset, the impulsive scale passages (Beethoven's treatment of scales is a study in itself), the shadow of a tune (for the substance of the melody does not appear until the piano has had time to consider it) which is introduced at bar 49 in a distant key, the improvisatory nature of the piano writing just after the half-way mark, the sequences of highly coloured chords in the piano, command even the most negligent ear. But high spirits are not excluded, and the final rondo of this concerto, based on a theme which carries faint echoes of Bohemia, is a youthful *jeu d'esprit*.

The second concerto is less rewarding, if only because the thematic material seems, in comparison with the companion works, trite. In Mozart one looks forward from conventional opening gambits to the play of intellect which they stimulate. In Beethoven one expects that each statement shall be urgent, or significant. Yet in the *adagio* of this concerto one cannot do other than pause before the breadth of the music. Herein there is time to stand and stare.

This movement, however, is not to be compared with the *largo* of the third concerto in C minor. This is in the far distant key of E major and the contrast between these keys is the first cause of wonderment. But as the piano alone develops the spacious theme the keys change and, before long, the music is temporarily in the key of G major. This is the dominant of C minor—so, although far out at sea, we are kept in touch with land. The entry of muted strings, the pearly decorations of woodwind solos by piano arpeggios, the delicate scale passages—which, though exquisitely decorative, serve a functional purpose in guiding the ear towards the harmonic progressions, make this movement a poetic experience. At the end the beauty is shattered, by a sharp fortissimo chord.

But it is in the first movement of the concerto that drama lies, and all within the pregnant rhythm of the opening bars. When this work was composed the *Sonata Pathétique* lay behind, and the fifth symphony was still some way ahead. But there is a connection between all three works, for Beethoven frequently cast his dramatic thought in the key of C minor.

In the fourth concerto the convention of the opening orchestral *ritornello* was dispersed. The piano enters at once with a theme completely at variance with any preconceptions regarding the character of first themes in concertos; for it is quiet and serene. And the serenity is enhanced when, a few bars later, the orchestral strings arrive in the warm key of B major. (Notice in Beethoven, as also in Haydn, the frequency with which keys at a distance of a third from each other alternate.) This movement shares with the opening movement of the violin concerto a ruminative quality that flowers from the first bars. To this the second movement—a dialogue between piano and orchestra—is corrective: for here lies a terse, gripping statement for strings in octaves to dominate the text. But against the strings is the answering gentleness of the piano: *una corda, molto espressivo*.

In the final rondo the strings take their leave of the dramatic in the fine-edged rhythmic opening. Thereafter the rondo is charmingly discursive but never irrelevant. This is the first of Beethoven's concertos in which the last movement is a worthy companion to the others. In the earlier works the rondo was present according to prescription, but was ill-at-ease in the company of allied movements that had developed so greatly.

In the fourth concerto there are neither trumpets nor drums. In the fifth the orchestra is back to what was then normal symphonic structure, with its complement of brass and percussion. The influence exercised on the concerto by the trumpets, horns, and drums is considerable and their imperious tone quality (unconsciously one is bound to the concept of brass and drums as symbolic of regality) may well seem to underwrite the popular idealization of the concerto as 'The Emperor'. Consider the blaze of the three chords with which the full orchestra sets off the compelling prelude with which the pianist commences. (This is another unconventional way of beginning; but once again the formal outlines of concerto are considered in relation to the character of the music.) Note the horn calls which are heard behind the first theme delivered by the strings, and the irradiation of the first climax by the springing arpeggios of the trumpets; the manner in which the horn, in major tonality, answers the interrogatory minor interlude of strings, clarinet, and bassoon. Below the horns the drums maintain the rhythm of the previous sections, thus unifying the elements. More than once towards the end of the first movement either one or two horns only are heard against the piano.

The slow movement, with its immortal melody, is characteristically put into the far-away tonality of B major. It is the horns which at the end fuse the second to the third movement. The last half-dozen bars of the slow movement deserve the closest aural scrutiny. The chord of B major is strongly emphasized. It dwindles to an octave B in the bassoons. They, dropping half a tone, hand over to the horns, and the pivotal note is B flat. This we feel (for the horns have, in the first movement, made a considerable point of B flat) is where we have been before. As we reflect, the piano deals out a spacious, uplifting sequence of E flat chords. These, for the present, are in the distance. But, says Beethoven, *attacca il Rondo*; and the pianist flies away with the exhilaration of the finale. In the background, the only orchestral contribution are the horns. From time to time the trumpets and the horns appear to gild the edge of the dynamic rhythm; but, towards the end, it is the drum, solitary in support of the piano, which most catches the ear.

In listening to a piano concerto it is generally thought considerate to concentrate attention on the soloist. Occasionally, however, I am all for studying—as here—the contribution made to the whole by less conspicuous participants. The glory of the great classical composers is in the inevitability of every note.

As we go through the 'Emperor' the procession of themes is amazing, and despite the figuration of the pianoforte and the harmonic distances travelled (for we are taken as far as B minor) the influence of the principal themes is never absent.

The fifth concerto, like the 'Emperor's Hymn' of Haydn, was associated with the painful days of 1809, when the French army was in occupation of Vienna. Haydn, it will be recalled, was carried to his piano by a French officer and requested to play his hymn tune. Beethoven, however, was in the throes of composition, amid, he wrote, 'a disturbing wild life around me; nothing but drums, cannons, men, misery of all sorts'. The concerto may or may not appear to reflect externals (that is a matter of individual feeling), but it represents certainly the indomitable urge of the great artist to 'create, to vanquish his fate'.

Both the fourth and fifth concertos were dedicated to Beethoven's remarkable patron, friend, and pupil, the Archduke Rudolph.

CHORAL FANTASIA · It is a little unorthodox to rate more than moderately Beethoven's most irregular work—the *Choral Fantasia*, but, since it is excellent fun to take part in, I recommend it to amateur societies. The woodwind writing of the variations, which constitute a major part of the work, is difficult, but it is unlikely that anybody could make a greater mess of the work than was made at its first production in Vienna in 1808. Things got into such a state that a halt had to be called, and a fresh start made. This concert was the last at which Beethoven himself played.

The beginning of this work is a fantasia for piano. This, at the first performance, was extemporized by Beethoven. The end of the work is a choral setting of an indifferent poem in praise of music. The chorus parts are agreeable to many singers, consisting of numerous high and loud notes in elementary rhythm. The whole is surprisingly effective, and not unnaturally associated with the Choral symphony.

VIOLIN CONCERTO · Sir Herbert Read somewhere observes that 'the real function of art is to express *feeling* and transmit *understanding*'. That seems a criterion by which one may judge Beethoven, and of all his works in concerto style it seems to me that the violin concerto is that which comes nearest to Read's definition.

Franz Clement, for whom Beethoven composed the violin concerto, was a remarkable artist. He was the best violinist in Vienna, soloist to the Emperor and conductor of the new Theater an der Wien. He was the friend of Haydn and Spohr, and had a phenomenal memory. Having heard Haydn's *Creation* he was able to make a piano score from memory. His tone was sweet rather than powerful, his intonation impeccable. He was a fine virtuoso, but also a fine musician. Beethoven's concerto is essentially a musician's concerto, one in which no player can be unaware of the activities of another. Ernest Walker commented unkindly on soloists who evaded this obligation: 'It is the *cheval de bataille* of all violinists; and if it has suffered even more than most classical concertos from the caprices of soloists who apparently consider any knowledge of other parts than their own entirely superfluous, not even the worst playing can hide the grandeur and beauty of every page.'

Grandeur and beauty are in the first two bars: in the admonition of the drums (whose five-note rhythm commands the entire first movement), and the serene chording and phrasing of the woodwind. The dramatic and the lyrical are clearly defined, and the varied placing of the inaugural rhythmic pattern intensifies the former. For instance, the first utterance of the first violins is of this pattern, but on an alien D sharp, anticipating later deviations from tonal compatability. There is, too, the impact of the full orchestra at the twenty-eighth bar. But here, as in the associated passages which occur later, there is nothing of tyranny. The music is under control, and the firm hand that so controls this aspect is similarly evident in the other, lyrical facet. The second tune of the movement, rising upward, is a singer's tune; that is to say, the listener with any urge to sing will find it irresistible. And it is the singing quality that is enhanced by the treatment by the solo violin. Of this violin part, and without disrespect to Vaughan Williams, one feels that it is the quintessence of Meredith's *Lark Ascending*: or, if you prefer, of Shelley's *Skylark*.

In the first movement it is clear that the solo part is a natural growth. There are no mere decorative flourishes, but each gesture is rooted in the character of the music. This inevitability continues into the *larghetto*; a solemn, mystical example of Beethoven's concept of a slow movement, but, at the same time, intimate and endearing. It is sometimes thought not quite proper to send musicians away to read poetry, but Shelley's *Spirit of Solitude* has something of Beethoven's mood:

> *Her voice was like the voice of his own soul*
> *Heard in the calm of thought; its music long,*
> *Like woven sounds of streams and breezes, held*
> *His inmost sense suspended in its web*
> *Of many-coloured woof and shifting hues.*

Shelley and Beethoven belonged to the same age and, conscious of the spirit of the age, it is hardly surprising that the attitudes of both overlapped. This, for example, is the continuation of the Shelley quotation:

> *Knowledge and truth and virtue were her theme,*
> *And lofty hopes of divine liberty . . .*

If that is not within Beethoven's music it was at least within his mind when he wrote his music.

And so to the rondo, which, as in the last of the piano concertos, is attacked at once. Here all is geniality. But the high spirits are still disciplined so that the pre-eminent grace of the first movement still casts its spell.

INTERPRETATIVE GENIUS OF JOACHIM · It was universally recognized that Joachim's greatness as an artist was never more evident than when he played this concerto. We may read Bernard Shaw's opinion, and take note of the castigation of Ysaÿe.

'Joachim, whose cadenzas, by the bye, are much better than

Ysaÿe's, takes his place beside the conductor and his orchestral colleagues as the interpreter of Beethoven, whose supremacy he never obscures for a moment. But who can think of Beethoven, or even of music, whilst Ysaÿe is Titanically emphasizing himself and his stupendous accomplishment, elbowing aside the conductor, eclipsing the little handful of an orchestra which he thinks sufficient for a concert in St James's Hall, and all but shewing Beethoven the door?'

The virtuoso temperament which, abetted by audiences avid for sensational performance, all but showed Beethoven the door grew increasingly unhappy in the limits of classical concerto. It fell to Brahms to attempt to re-establish classical integrity. And Joachim, the great exponent of Beethoven, was also the pioneer of Brahms. The cadenza commonly played in the violin concerto of Brahms is that of Joachim (even though there are at least seventeen cadenzas by other hands); and it is to this concerto that we may now turn.

[JOHANNES BRAHMS (1833–1897)

VIOLIN CONCERTO · What might be called the doctrine of inevitability is illustrated in legend by the account of the birth of the goddess Pallas Athene. She, fully grown and armed, sprang to life from the brain of her father Zeus. There are works of art which give some similar impression; among them is Brahms's violin concerto. Yet, as was often the case with Brahms, the apparently inevitable quality of the music was the result of many re-writings and many consultations with Joachim. Nor was the music well received. It was, said some who preferred concertos of a more demonstrative character, a concerto against the violin.

How wrong critics can be is demonstrated by the progress of this concerto since 1879, when, on New Year's Day, it was performed in Leipzig. It is now one of the few essential violin concertos.

Brahms was a lyrical composer, one of the half-dozen greatest song-writers of all time, and in common with Beethoven in his violin concerto, he dignifies the violin (the same is true of the sonatas) by inducing it to sing. It is this quality which gives to the slow movement—*adagio*—sufficient significance to balance the outer movements. For here, where there is but one melody which extends through the movement, is the climax of song. Connoisseurs of woodwind scoring will regard the opening of the *adagio*, the melody lying in the oboe, with abiding affection and will note the manner in which this instrumentation sets off the contrasting violin arabesque. Calm and deep peace: this is as characteristic of Brahms as of Tennyson. This is the mood of the *adagio*, but not unaltered, for at the centre of the music is an agitated section in F sharp minor. Again the woodwind are employed prominently to introduce the section.

Those who admit a taste, however slender, for the sensational will find their pleasure more readily in the last movement—*allegro giocoso, ma non troppo vivace*, in which the violin immediately turns out a fiery tune of *tzigane* quality. In the first movement Brahms, thoroughly classical in presentation, engages sympathy by the row of melodies which are first outlined by the orchestra. As in the second symphony there is a pastoral character which is in no sense diminished by the didactic skill of the composer. The manner of varying and developing the themes, and of using them contrapuntally, shows Brahms's seriousness of approach and his craftsmanship; but the quality is that of a poet and not of a pedant.

PIANO CONCERTOS · When he wrote the violin concerto Brahms put aside his work on the second of the piano concertos, that in B flat. This was begun in 1878, but not completed until 1881. This concerto was a rarity in being formed in four movements, the second a *scherzo*; a rough-edged piece in D minor, marked *allegro appassionato*, within which, however, is a lively trio in D major. The organization of the movement, as of the whole concerto, is complex and subtle. The greatness of the work is due to the fact that nothing is irrelevant.

The slow movement, for example, is exactly complementary to the unexpected *scherzo*, whereas it would follow oddly immediately after the opening movement. It was sometimes said in former times that Brahms was no great orchestrator. The point is that his scoring is at one with the character of his music, and that he unfailingly colours it with what, in the long run, is the appropriate colour. So it is that the third movement of the work begins with a melody for solo cello which, as in the case of the woodwind in the violin concerto, creates the atmosphere in which the movement henceforth moves. In Brahms, as in Beethoven, one works from the heart of the music, outwards: this is the index to the suffusing spirit of Romanticism. In a letter to Joachim Brahms once indicated the trouble it was to him to compose a slow movement to his satisfaction.

'I wish', he wrote, 'I could write a really satisfactory *Adagio*.' This was in 1857, and in respect of the first piano concerto. From this it will also be seen that concertos occupied his attention for a great part of his career.

We may indeed go further back, for it was in 1854—Brahms then being only twenty-one—that Otto Julius Grimm, composer and pianist, remarked to Joachim that Brahms had written three movements of a sonata for two pianos. Brahms was dissatisfied with the music as it stood and recast the first movement as for a symphony. But he had third thoughts and a piano concerto began to emerge. In 1856 the *adagio* and rondo were added to the movement from the sonata. (The second movement of this was remoulded into the second section of the *German Requiem*.)

In music of the Romantic period influences from outside music may often be descried. So it is in the case of the slow movement of the first piano concerto. One might guess this, for there is present the feeling of choral music, orchestra and piano answering each other like two groups of voices in a motet for double-choir. In fact the *adagio* bore an inscription: 'Benedictus qui venit in nomine Domini.' Perhaps this remains from a mass designed in commemoration of Robert Schumann—he died in 1856—to whom Brahms was devoted. The movement has a nobility towards which Schumann also aspired and of which, in this context, he would have approved.

From this point one is returned to the equally noble, and moving, second tune in the first movement (marked *poco piu moderato*). If this represents one aspect of Brahms then so does the opening of the movement another: the tempestuous. *Sturm and Drang* was consistent in German thought from the time of Schiller,

Goethe, and Herder; and Brahms, the disciple of Beethoven, is rarely far from its influence. So the concerto opens, together with the first and third symphonies, in this vein. Brahms was a great organizer of musical material and his talent for organization is nowhere better shown than in the recapitulation of this movement. (The recapitulation is that final part of a movement following classical precept in which the themes of the exposition are re-peated in their original order, but going towards the tonic key, and not away from it.) The massive theme which was at first in the orchestra is now peremptorily delivered by the piano, with a totally surprising chord of E major above low held notes in the orchestral bass; then it is broken up and tucked imitatively between piano and orchestra. To the end this motiv is dominating; which only serves to show up the *poco piu moderato* section, now in D major, in greater contrast.

The rondo, rough but thoughtful, contains a vast amount of musical interest, not least of all in the fugal working out which in mid-course and in the coda recalls the devotion of Brahms to the music of Bach. At the end it is major tonality that prevails, and so the tension of tonality is resolved. It was this movement that Elgar took as a model when he began to sketch a final move-ment for his—incomplete and unpublished—piano concerto.

Brahms, pianist as well as composer, played the first concerto in Hanover on 22 January 1859, and five days later in the Gewand-haus in Leipzig. Brahms wrote to Joachim: 'It did not go badly; I played considerably better than in Hanover and the orchestra was excellent. But the first rehearsal failed to produce any effect on the musicians or the audience. At the second rehearsal there were no listeners and not a muscle moved on the faces of the players. . . . At the performance the first and second movements produced no effect whatsoever and at the end there was only a little desultory applause which was immediately suppressed.'

The way of a composer is never easy: all music begins under the handicap of being 'modern music'.

The right of Brahms to be ranked as a classical composer is often granted because he was a conservative in the matter of structure. Moving away from the tintinabulations of the virtuoso

E

school and from the idea that virtue resided in the abolition of separate movements he found that the way in which Beethoven expressed himself was congenial to him also. But 'classical' is more a matter of character. A classic, in whatever art, is comprehensive, but finally immutable. There is something of Milton in Brahms, and as is Milton to Shakespeare, so, perhaps, is Brahms to Beethoven.

V. Pianoforte Concertos

ROMANTIC IDEALS · About classical art there is a certain aura of inscrutability. In this, of course, lies the perpetual fascination exercised on the minds of succeeding generations by the classic works whether of literature, painting, sculpture, or music. The field of art is bounded on the one side by the ideal, on the other by the real. In nine-tenths of the music of Mozart we are, it would seem, nearer to the ideal than to the real; thus it is that he is the classical composer *par excellence*. One is readily aware of a capacity for holding back—indeed, restraint is one of the qualifying principles of classicism. Mozart expressed himself on this point in a sentence which Elgar used to keep on his desk as remedial for his apolaustic instincts. 'The passions', Mozart wrote to his father, 'whether violent or otherwise must never be expressed to disgust—and music, even in the most terrific situations, never give pain to the ear, but ever delight it and remain Music.' From another sphere may be recalled an apt sentence by Ingres, the French classical painter: 'a thing well drawn is always well enough painted.'

Looking back across the vast acres of musical colour in Ravel and Debussy, Stravinsky and Strauss, Tchaikovsky and Mahler, Wagner and Berlioz, one may well return to the restraint of necessarily less effusive designers with some relief. So it is that the harpsichord and the baroque-style organ are once again in vogue.

The piano, perhaps, is not now quite the influence that it was. One does not, for instance, notice, in a young lady's playing, as did George Eliot in her Rosamond Vincey, that 'a hidden sound seemed to be flowing forth from her fingers'. Unless, that is, there is a particular interest in the young lady quite apart from pianistic considerations. The soul is at the moment out of commission in the arts; but to understand the quality of the nineteenth-century concerto some belief in it needs to be revived. Chopin and Schumann, Liszt and Tchaikovsky, to a lesser extent Grieg and César Franck, were the great exponents of soul-music as represented in pianoforte concertos.

The pianoforte was the ideal romantic period instrument, putting dreams at the tips of the fingers. Through its variety of tone-colour, its dynamic range, its evanescent quality it invited self-expression. From Hummel to Delius a long list might be drawn up of distinguished composers who tended to seek out their music, esoterically, at the keyboard.

On the other hand the pianoforte had its public character. In tonal brilliance and percussive violence it could command the attention of the multitude. With the piano to hand, therefore, the composer who enjoyed the mechanical excellences of the nineteenth-century instrument could either soliloquize or rant.

❡ JOHAN HUMMEL (1778–1837) AND IGNAZ MOSCHELES (1794–1870) · When Beethoven died an inevitable reaction set in against his music, and by 1830 his works, together with those of Mozart and Haydn, were regarded less favourably in Vienna, Leipzig, Paris, and London than was previously the case. There were those who carried on the 'classical' tradition—Hummel and Moscheles, for example. But not even they—musicians of great integrity—could escape the craze for brilliance, for fantasy, for 'coquetry' that affected music, especially pianoforte music, in the twenty years following the end of the Napoleonic Wars. It was the period in which, as Schumann said, 'legions of girls were in love with Czerny'. One day, perhaps, Moscheles will be revived. If so his concerto of 1823, of which the finale is based on *The British Grenadiers*, might again be aired, and the two more notable essays in Romantic style—the 'Fantastic' and 'Pathetic' concertos.

❡ JOHN FIELD (1782–1837) · From the same period might also be revived the concertos of John Field, that intemperate Irish genius whose poetry greatly influenced Chopin. In his outer movements Field wrote freshly-complexioned music of some wit and with Schubertian tints in the harmony, while in his slow movements he cultivated the atmospherics of his own charming 'nocturnes'. The orchestra, however, was not regarded as of any great significance and, such was the overpowering influence of the instrument that, even in the storm and tempest passages of the fifth concerto—*L'Incendie par l'orage*—the effects are achieved by the inclusion in the score of a second pianoforte.

❡ CARL MARIA VON WEBER (1786–1826) · Almost exactly contemporary with John Field was Weber, whose genius, if not dissimilar to that of Field, is of a higher order. It is also more various. In Weber is the exhilaration of the first phase of musical Romanticism, a conspicuous sense of adventure, a delight in instrumental sonorities, and a finely varied technical equipment. In his *Concertstück* (1821) he summarized in concerto style one side of Romantic philosophy; it is an evocation of the middle ages. Prompted by a literary plan the *Concertstück* departs from the conventional concerto pattern. There are four movements— *Larghetto affetuoso, Allegro passionato, Tempo di marcia*, and *Presto giocoso*, which are continuous.

No composer before Wagner expressed such atmosphere with greater vividness than Weber, and the *Concertstück*—which crosses operatic genius with virtuoso piano technique—is as palatable as a chapter by Scott.

❡ FELIX MENDELSSOHN (1809–1847) · Ten years after the appearance of Weber's *Concertstück* came the first of Mendelssohn's piano concertos, that in G minor. Weber had been somewhat doubtful of the wisdom of launching a work in minor tonality into the sea of 'grand concertos' in major keys that flooded the market. (His previous piano concerto had been in C major and E flat major.) But by 1830 the tendency of German romanticism was towards melancholy. Thus Mendelssohn, as Schumann, found it convenient to notice, by tonal reference, the prevailing sentiment.

It was not, however, in Mendelssohn's nature to explore the darker reaches of the unconscious. There was too much of the classic in him, and there is no doubt that the quotation from Mozart relating to the discipline of the passions would accurately have expressed his point of view. It is in the slow movements of his concertos that discipline appears as repressive, for neither in the piano concertos nor in the violin concerto do the middle movements depart sufficiently far from equability to stir much response from the ardent mind. Songs without words are admirable for domestic use, but inadequate for public exhibition.

Mendelssohn's extraordinary facility as pianist provoked from him some of the best of *bravura* music, and the final movements of the concerto in G minor and D minor, and of the unjustly neglected *Serenade and Allegro giojoso*, are brilliant tokens of Mendelssohn's high-spirited fancy. In each case there is more than a trace of the influence of Weber, but it is always music for music's sake and the dominant characteristic of the style is economy.

Although Mendelssohn was averse from literary programmes for his music, it is not difficult from time to time to sense an awareness of literary values behind the music. Thus in the first piano concerto the first movement runs into the second through a highly coloured rhythmic figure, in octaves, given by wood-wind and dealt with in turn by brass and strings. The Crusaders, perhaps, are in the wings. The same figure is used again in this concerto to unite the second with the third movement.

Thus we are aware that Mendelssohn was intent on unity of design. The last two of Beethoven's concertos as well as Weber's *Concertstück* were partly responsible. But there was another reason. Mendelssohn's sense of propriety was upset frequently by the manners of audiences, who, in his day, would disturb any sequence of musical ideas to applaud those which they approved. Thus a concerto with three movements and including a couple of cadenzas was likely to gain five rounds of applause. Marks of disapproval, on the other hand, were not unknown either. By cutting out cadenzas (there are none in the piano concertos) and by running one movement into the next Mendelssohn not only reformed concerto style but also audience deportment. There are other formal marks of originality. In the exposition of the piano concertos the thematic material is delivered once only, divided between orchestra and soloist.

In some ways Mendelssohn is the great business executive of music. His ideals were fitted into the limits of the practical. He is for ever astonishingly competent. Thus to the concerto and the *Serenade and Allegro giojoso* should be added the *Capriccio brillante* and the *Rondo brillante*, exciting pieces with no palpable defects of design, as always illuminated by striking and pellucid orchestration, and delightfully calculated to stimulate an appreciation of efficiency. For inspiration—or what is generally taken for inspiration—one should look elsewhere.

❦ FREDERIC CHOPIN (1810–1849) · There are two concertos by Chopin, for instance, which are far more personal—and therefore more romantic—than anything that Mendelssohn wrote in this form. But they lack the sureness of exposition that characterized Mendelssohn. As a boy in Warsaw Chopin was well away from the main stream of European music. His ambition, at the age of twenty, to compose pianoforte concertos was hindered by the inadequacy of the models available to him. Beethoven was not played. It was the works of Kalkbrenner, Ries, Hummel, and Field that were in vogue in the capital of Poland. And since in their concertos the orchestra was relegated to a subordinate role it is not surprising that the impressionable Chopin, who had met Hummel in 1828, also put most of his eggs into one basket. The two concertos, in E minor (dedicated to Kalkbrenner, who was celebrated as pianist and teacher in Paris) and F minor, are distinguished by brilliance and poetry in the piano parts, but marred by a desultory sense of structure and indifferent orchestration. It is, however, only fair to point out that the dramatic episode of

the slow movement of the F minor concerto has one touch of
genius in the scoring, as the piano recitative in A flat minor is set
off by *tremolo* strings above pizzicato double basses. These concertos of Chopin have been subjected to re-editing. Carl Tausig
re-orchestrated that in E minor, and Carl Klindworth that in F
minor, and both made other 'improvements'.

❡ ROBERT SCHUMANN (1810–1856) · Robert Schumann, of the
same age as Chopin and a year younger than Mendelssohn, is one
of the most attractive and, at the same time, one of the saddest
figures in musical history. His imaginative power, stimulated by
a lifelong study of the masters of Romantic literature and conditioned by his psychotic nature, was intense; his acquaintance with
music, both ancient and modern, comprehensive; his generosity to
fellow musicians remarkable; his ideals high. He disliked virtuosity for its own sake and found in the piano the proper medium
for the expression of his thoughts. Perpetually, however, Schumann was haunted by dark thoughts—which eventually led to a
complete mental collapse and early death.

It is the dark thoughts which give to so much of his music its
characteristic *Nachtstück* atmosphere. On the other hand, as in
the last movement of the piano concerto, joviality is present. But
on reflection the joviality will be found to have a forced quality:
it belongs to a man who tried to conquer his fate by throwing
himself, from time to time, into the midst of German heartiness.

The last section of Schumann's A minor piano concerto is an
immensely popular movement. In its thematic material—in the
hail-fellow-well-met first tune (bar 109) and the comic, rhythmic-
ally eccentric, second tune (bar 189)—there is, indeed, this
quality of heartiness which was so much applauded in the community in which Schumann lived. This is a fine virile piece of
writing, more forceful than brilliant, being less note-full than the
general run of *brillante* pieces. In the light of Schumann's biography it is, however, a movement with a hidden poignancy.
This is not Schumann's true nature: it is the mask that sometimes
he compelled himself to wear.

There is no reason why music should not be enjoyed for itself,
without biographical annotation. But Schumann, seeing in his

music a projection of himself, is a special case. Speaking quite personally, there are few composers whose minds are so clearly defined by their music as Schumann. Thus we return from the final section of the concerto to the preceding intermezzo, with its gentle, somewhat uncertain, opening theme in F major, divided between piano and strings, and the contrasting cello melody in C major (bar 29). The wide intervals of the second melody, characteristic of Schumann and later Elgar, are suggestive of a desire for affection that marked Schumann's personality. So, in Schumann, we begin to see what we might clearly have noted in Weber and Chopin—that melodies in the Romantic period are important in themselves; more important in fact than their working out.

Weber, Mendelssohn, and Chopin, as well as the majority of their lesser contemporaries, played their own music. Schumann did not. After 1832 (the year in which he damaged his hand and thereby terminated his brief career as pianist) his works were written for Clara Wieck, whom he married in 1840.

During the first year of his marriage Schumann was exceedingly prolific. During that year, in which Clara encouraged him to believe that his powers were in no way inferior to those of any living composer, not even the idolized Mendelssohn, large works began to take shape. For ten years at least the possibility that he might compose a piano concerto had been in mind. Now he set about a single movement. It was to be no display piece, but rather an expression of poetic feeling. Thus he termed what now is the first movement of Opus 54 a *Phantasie*, which links the work with the great C major *Phantasie* of 1838 and also with the literary works of E. T. A. Hoffmann, from whom Schumann transferred the title to music.

This movement, in A minor, is an ingenious mixture of sonata and variation. It is, paradoxically, both compact and expansive; compact in that the woodwind melody which succeeds the brief, eruptive flourish by the soloist is transferred into C major and made to serve as a 'second subject' and also used as the main-spring of subsequent action; expansive in the scoring (unusually lucid for Schumann) and in the range of keys. One of the most beautiful points in the score is at bar 157 where the pianoforte sets out a more languid version of the main theme in the distant key of A flat, the sensibility of which transformation is enhanced by the adjacent entry of clarinet supported by flutes. In this movement there is a cadenza, an earnest passage in the middle of the keyboard (where so much of Schumann's keyboard music lies) and anticipating somewhat the *chorale* manner of César Franck. After the cadenza an *allegro molto* in quick march time flies to a lively conclusion. So much was the *Phantasie*, of which Schumann's publishers had, at first, a poor opinion. Schumann, in fact, was at that time regarded as dangerously modern and often unintelligible. Since he was so cavalier with the old forms— which were sometimes regarded as an end in themselves—and since he discouraged musical pyrotechnics, one can understand the suspicion with which he was regarded.

After four years the *Phantasie* was joined by the two interlinked movements, provisionally entitled *Andantino and Rondo*, which complete the concerto. It will be noticed that the prevailing theme of the first movement appears prominently at the end of the intermezzo (which runs without break into the finale), and thus imposes a great sense of unity.

❡ FRANZ LISZT (1811–1886) · In the early 1840's the Schumanns lived in Leipzig: a city with an ancient musical tradition and at that time boasting of its connection with Mendelssohn, who directed the concerts at the Gewandhaus and also the new Conservatorium. Leipzig became a place of pilgrimage and, as will be seen, a good proportion of the more respectable composers of the last half of the nineteenth century had their affiliations there. During the time that Schumann lived there—he edited a musical journal which exerted a considerable influence on the progressives—many great performers appeared at the Gewandhaus. The greatest, perhaps, was Liszt who, although a year younger than Schumann, was already a legend.

His Hungarian origins, his striking appearance, his magnifical manner, his romantic way of life, the general impression of genius that he gave would all have commanded respect if he had been no more than a moderate performer. But, as it happened, he was, by general consent, the greatest pianist that had ever been known. There is a finely-drawn pen-picture by George Eliot, who heard Liszt at Weimar in 1854: 'For the first time in my life I beheld real inspiration—for the first time I heard the true tones of the piano. He played one of his own compositions. . . . There was nothing strange or excessive about his manner. His manipulation of the instrument was quiet and easy, and his face was simply grand—the lips compressed and the head thrown a little backward. When the music expressed quiet rapture or devotion, a sweet smile flitted over his features; when it was triumphant, the nostrils dilated. There was nothing petty or egoistic to mar the picture.'

Some part of Liszt's glamour lay in this affectation of modesty —apparently the exquisite modesty of one who knows himself to be great. He was a superb actor, and it is the histrionic side of his personality which lives on in those of his works which have survived his death. The concerto in E flat is no exception. After the orchestral introduction of four bars the piano enters imperiously, with striking octaves, and plunges very soon into a commanding cadenza. To the end of the concerto there is hardly a point where the listener is not aware of the composer's complete mastery of pianoforte technique. Even now the 'new scales of ornament, the new gradations of tone, the flashing, scintillating rapidity and the power of endurance' that so captivated the ear a hundred years ago are compelling enough.

Then there are other factors: the 'popular' quality of the introductory theme, the conspicuous use of this theme throughout the concerto, the vivid harmonic and orchestral coloration, the percussive character that is most conspicuously symbolized by the significant role of the triangle in the *Allegretto vivace* which is the third section of the work. Pedants found these innovations alarming. Especially the use of the triangle which, thought to be almost indecent, gave rise to the offensive use of the term 'Triangle Concerto'. This was the brainwave of a Viennese critic. In fact the percussive quality of this concerto—and of other works by Liszt—is common ground between him and contemporary music; and it all came from his love for Hungarian music.

The E flat concerto is in four interlinked sections, as a symphony. Previously a number of composers had attempted a
unification of concerto form, but Liszt was a little more thorough.
He centred his work on the motto theme which is given at the
outset. It is a dramatic theme—by now because of its frequent
imitation identifiable with a host of bloodthirsty tunes which lie
in the hinterland of film music: the sort of theme that immediately
suggests something 'real'. This, some of us may feel, is music we
can 'understand'. When we have got to this point we are faced
with the words which Liszt used to sing to his motto theme: 'Das
versteht Ihr alle nicht' ('None of you understand this'). The
romantic loved his cloak of mystery. And this is evident in the
quasi adagio, second section, of the concerto in the key of B major.
With some acknowledgment to Chopin in the figuration this is
a nocturne, and accompanied by muted strings.

The colour scheme is beautiful, but it is difficult to enthuse
about the melodic quality. In fact Liszt was no great melodist.
This was part of the price he paid for pursuing the motto theme
idea so relentlessly. The nocturne theme, for instance, appears in
the final section of the concerto, *allegro marziale animato*, and
sounds very much better in the new than in the old guise.

Since music which once was 'modern' is now invariably given
an intermediate station on the line of musical progress it is worth
noting that the first performance of the E flat concerto, in Weimar
on 17 February 1855, was conducted by Berlioz, whose mark may
be frequently seen in the orchestral works of Liszt.

The second piano concerto of Liszt, in A major, is, perhaps,
more interesting than the first as it is also more perplexing. Here
is a concerto in one movement with little connection with any
previous essays in solo concerto manner. It is a word picture,
summarized by the sectional directions—*adagio*, *allegro agitato*,
allegro moderato, a march, *un poco meno allegro*, and a concluding
allegro animato. Although neither of these concertos bears descriptive titles they might well do so, so colour-conscious are they
and so akin to the symphonic poem of which Liszt was the
originator.

The originality of a composer is to be judged not by the look of his music, but by its sound. Therefore what seems of special interest on paper—as the thematic manipulation of the Liszt school—tends to hold less interest to the ear, and the originality of the method is accordingly mitigated. This, perhaps, is where Liszt compares unfavourably with Tchaikovsky, whose genius lay in the disposition of his sounds. But there is one work by Liszt which should not be overlooked: the *Dance of Death*. This, a set of variations on the plainsong hymn *Dies Irae* (Day of Wrath) for piano and orchestra, was composed in 1849 but was not performed for the first time until more than thirty years later.

The Dance of Death was inspired by a series of wall paintings in Pisa thought to have been done by Andrea Orcagna. Liszt gives to his music an unearthly quality of mingled horror and fantasy. The rhythmic layout and the scoring are terrific, and the piano takes on a hard, sardonic character, which sharpens the angles of fear far more than the xylophone in Saint-Saëns' *Danse Macabre*. Liszt the man was half saint and half devil: in the *Dance of Death* the diabolic rings terribly true.

The *Dies Irae* melody has served numerous composers since Berlioz introduced it into the 'Witches' Sabbath' of his *Fantastic Symphony*—the pioneer work in the cult of 'horror' in concert-room music. The most prominent recent use of the *Dies Irae* within a work is in the *Paganini Rhapsody* of Rachmaninov. This also is a set of variations, but on a theme (the same theme used previously by both Schumann and Brahms) from Paganini's violin caprice in A minor, which in itself bears a superficial thematic resemblance to the *Dies Irae*.

Rachmaninov in his concertos is directly in the virtuoso tradition of Liszt—Rachmaninov was the last composer-virtuoso in the general manner—but is also in a separate line of descent from the Russian nationalist school and from Tchaikovsky. No one, except, perhaps, Brahms, was unaffected by the music of Liszt within the second half of the nineteenth century; but some were affected more than others.

'It is impossible to believe the force and the magical prestige that attached to the name of Liszt in the eyes of all young musicians during the first years of the Imperial epoch of Napoleon III.

This name of Liszt, sounding strangely enough, in any case, to us Frenchmen, sharp and whistling in its sound, like a sword cutting the air, traversed and sliced in two by the "Z" of the Slavs, as if by the furrow of the lightning.' The 'furrow of the lightning': by putting aside, temporarily, our knowledge of twentieth-century music, by relating the music of Liszt to that of the other composers of the 1860's and 1870's we can appreciate what Camille Saint-Saëns felt when he recollected Liszt in his *Portraits et Souvenirs*. Saint-Saëns idolized the music of Liszt and in his own music may often be seen the result of his affection. In particular he followed Liszt's example in writing symphonic poems (of which *Omphale's Spinning Wheel* is the most familiar).

❡ CAMILLE SAINT–SAËNS (1835–1921) · But Saint-Saëns was also a brilliant pianist and among his ten concertos there are five for piano. There is also the *Carnival of Animals*, for two pianos and small orchestra, a comedy piece with more to it—in its allusions —than at first meets the ear. Of the piano concertos two—the second in G minor and the fourth in C minor—still enjoy occasional revival.

❡ CÉSAR FRANCK (1822–1890) · César Franck also derived much from the music of Liszt. Belgian by birth, Franck was a mystic, and it was the quality of mysticism in Liszt (as well as his personal generosity, which was greatly encouraging to both Saint-Saëns and Franck) that captivated him. It was Franck's prerogative to dignify French music, to give to it a religious impulse and a patent sincerity that so strongly marked his own character. The harmonic manner and the structural freedom of Liszt attracted him; but he, to a greater degree than Saint-Saëns, was also influenced by the works of Bach. Indeed, through Mendelssohn, Schumann, Brahms, and Franck, Bach appears as one of the great liberating influences of the nineteenth century: and it puts him in a new light when it is realized that then he was regarded as a prophet of Romanticism.

César Franck, like Schumann, was influenced by the ruminative quality of Bach; the quality which gives to so much of the keyboard music the impression that the composer is thinking aloud. It is so in the *Symphonic Variations*, which Franck composed in

1885. This was not Franck's first essay in writing for piano and orchestra for, a year previously, he had composed the third of his symphonic poems—*Les Djinns*. This, based on a poem from Victor Hugo's *Les Orientales*, was very much in the manner of Liszt, even though the virtuoso element in the piano part was relatively subdued. After *Les Djinns* Franck turned to the *Prélude, Choral, et Fugue*, for piano solo, which was intended as an essay in the Bach style. The *Symphonic Variations* followed, and after that came the violin sonata, the *Prélude, Aria et Finale* for piano, and the symphony. Thus it was a prolific period.

The *Symphonic Variations* has affinities with all the works of the same period. The opening statement, by the strings, is dramatic in rhythm and chromatic character, comparing somewhat with the opening of Liszt's E flat major concerto. The exposition of the important paragraph at bar 100, by the piano, is texturally akin to the *choral* manner, and thematically to the slow movement of the symphony. In the brilliant finale there is again a recollection of the sheen of Liszt. Thus the complete work blends the two characteristics of later Romanticism—thoughtfulness and brilliance. In that these are resolved into a unity the work forms an impressive whole.

The pattern is interesting and lucid. There is an introduction, based on the initial statement by the strings and an appealing, falling, counter-theme by the piano, of which the feature is the interval of the augmented second from B sharp to A natural; the theme, delivered by the piano, which is followed by six variations; and a finale in the key of F sharp major in which the melancholy falling pattern from the introduction is transformed into a most ebullient motiv.

Often one is in mind of Schumann, for in writing variations Franck followed his example in avoiding the decorative treatment often given them and concentrating on the inner, personal qualities that he recognized beneath the surface of the melody. So the poetic nature of Franck's music emerges; and nowhere more conspicuously than in the nocturnal episode between [N] and [O].

❡ ANTON RUBINSTEIN (1829–1894) · Anton Rubinstein, who

conducted the first performance of the G minor concerto of Saint-Saëns in 1868, merits some notice; for, although our only acquaintance with his music is now likely to be through some chance contact with his salon music in an anthology of favourite pieces of the late nineteenth century, his place in the story of concerto is important. Rubinstein was the first of the great cosmopolitan Russian composer-virtuosi. Although he was first trained in Moscow he went to Paris, in 1839, drawn by the magic of Liszt's reputation. Benefiting from Liszt's counsel he diligently pursued his studies in composition for the next eight or nine years, at the same time increasing his fame as pianist by turns throughout Europe. In the 1850's and 60's he was celebrated all over Europe, and also in America. In 1862 he founded the St Petersburg Conservatory of Music of which he remained principal until 1867.

Rubinstein had little patience with the nationalist Russian school—his own compositions, which include five piano concertos, deriving from the style of Mendelssohn—and taught his pupils the virtues of the 'universal' (i.e. the German-Austrian) style as opposed to that which sought novelty in recourse to folk-music idiom. Among Rubinstein's pupils at St Petersburg was Tchaikovsky who, much under the influence of his master, set his face against the apparently narrow outlook of the school of Glinka, Dargomizhsky, Cui, Borodin, Balakirev, and Moussorgsky.

❡ PETER ILYITCH TCHAIKOVSKY (1840–1893) · It is not, however, style which initially interests us in the music of Tchaikovsky. As we hear either of the piano concertos, or any of the symphonies, we are aware of a rare capacity for direct emotional communication. This it is that perpetuates the music: it is alive in that as we hear it we, by a process of immersion, may live some part of our own lives through it.

Tchaikovsky was a neurotic. His biography is a saddening record of one who could not come to terms either with himself or with society. His salvation was music. 'Work', he wrote to Madame von Meck, 'saves me—work which is at the same time a pleasure. Thanks to a few successes which have fallen to my lot,

I have taken courage, and depressions, which used to amount to hallucinations and insanity, rarely visit me.'

By extreme perseverance Tchaikovsky acquired the technical equipment necessary for a composer. He was an inveterate student of other men's works, and his chief love was for Mozart. 'Under normal conditions', he once said, 'there is no hour of the day in which I cannot compose.' In this he was far different from, say, Schumann—the other outstandingly 'personal' composer of the century. It was the self-imposed discipline, together with a somewhat aristocratic distaste for nationalism, which gave to Tchaikovsky the outwardly classical features of his structures. The first piano concerto, for example, is a masterly piece of planning—except for one detail.

This concerto begins with one of the most impressive introductions in music. The four horns enter *fortissimo*, leading to vast chords from the piano, against which the violin and cellos in rich octaves continue what the horns had commenced. Irresistibly the piano presses forward into a cadenza. Thus early the soloist presents his credentials as a worthy duellist. The initial theme is delivered again, with added energy, by all the strings—apart from the double basses. Then it disappears, dissolving finally into a *pizzicato* shadow in cellos and horns. And this is the last that is heard of that splendid impetuous music. Thereafter the concerto pursues a formally correct course on independent lines. It is, writes Eric Blom, 'as though [one] were witnessing a performance of *Hamlet* in which the Prince of Denmark is killed by Polonius at the end of the first scene. It is this even more than its appearing in the wrong dress of B flat which makes Tchaikovsky's introduction, for all its magnificence, or at least magniloquence, one of the most baffling solecisms in the music of any great composer.'

After the introduction—which has served as background music to perhaps half-a-dozen films and has fathered that to many more —the remaining 557 bars of the first movement embrace almost the whole of the romantic hero conception. Life, urged the romantic, is a struggle against destiny: an unequal struggle, for the odds are always too heavy. At once Tchaikovsky plunges

F

into an ominous atmosphere, with a broken rhythmic figure—
now in the proper key of B flat minor—which is announced at
first by the piano alone. This idea carries on until, at bar 186, a
second theme is announced in the woodwind, to be repeated by
the piano. In this, with syncopation in each of the first two bars,
are rhythmic hesitations characteristic of the grief-laden aspect of
the music of the age. Similar features are also to be found in the
concertos of Rachmaninov. There is still one more melody to
come. After the piano has taken the second tune into a dark
cadence in C minor the first violins, muted, introduce a more
beneficent influence in the shape of a theme which undulates
within the limits of a seventh. The rest of the strings are muted—
the cellos and basses *pizzicato*—and, combined with contrasted
fifths from bassoons and horns, form the accompaniment. By
this point one is aware of Tchaikovsky's resource as an orchestrator, and the colours of the instrumentation become increasingly significant in expressing the emotional quality of the music.
The second theme returns with first flute and then oboe enhanc-
ing the character of the tune of the piano. Now the woodwind
as a group, above a drum roll becoming more and more intense,
and against triplet figuration in the piano, reach a great climax,
from which the piano proceeds through a cadenza-like interlude
to the central part of the movement.

For a time the development is carried on almost entirely by the
orchestra, but a series of truculent octaves, descending in four
note groups, give the cue to the soloist, who proceeds to show
how much more effective they can be in double octaves on the
keyboard. Now in command the piano undertakes a cadenza
which, reflecting on the character of the second tune, turns aside
to new but cognate thoughts rising uneasily in dialogue between
orchestra and piano above a held note in the basses and a drum
roll. The end of this section is signalized by another brief display
of power by the piano; and then follows the résumé of the whole
of the melodic material in a grand recapitulation in major tonality
which includes yet another cadenza—and this the most extensive
of all.

Writing of the concerto Tchaikovsky observed: 'Here we are

dealing with two equal opponents; the orchestra with its power, and inexhaustible variety of colour, opposed by the small but high-mettled piano, which often comes off victorious in the hands of a gifted executant'. In the first movement the honours are about even. That this is so is due to the resolution of the lay-out of the piano part, to the cadenzas which display what the piano can and the orchestra cannot do, and to the dramatic genius with which Tchaikovsky switches interest from one contestant to the other.

The slow movement, *andantino semplice*, is a nocturne; dignified in its beginning and its ending, fantastic in its *prestissimo* middle section. This is a most subtle example of colouring, and it is sufficient at first to follow the course the tune, which first appears in the flute, pursues through the score. At first the flute soars above the muted *pizzicato* chords of the strings. Then the piano takes up, as in the background the strings forsake *pizzicato* for *arco*. There follows a change of key—to D major—and a change of pattern as semi-quavers in oboe and clarinets weave a chain of sound above the bare fifths sounded by the bassoons. This is taken over by the piano, and, before long, the first bars of the first melody are half-remembered by horn, oboe, clarinet, and bassoon in turn. The key changes back to D flat major, and here two solo cellos return to the first theme in fuller form, until it is handed over to the oboe. The *prestissimo* section is carried along by the rapid figuration of the piano part, before which first violas and cellos, and then flute and oboe, present a melody said to have been of French origin and to have been introduced to Tchaikovsky by Désirée Artôt, to whom he was once engaged. A cadenza ends the *prestissimo* and returns the principal melody, now delivered by the piano. The end of the movement is lan-guorous; the strings have been muted throughout, and by now it is, perhaps, as in Shelley's *Spirit of Night:*

'Touching all with opiate wand.'

Although Tchaikovsky expressed himself against the national-ists he was by no means averse from infecting his own music with folk song. Thus in the first movement the theme which begins the movement proper is reputed to have been of popular Ukrainian origin. It was, they said, first heard by Tchaikovsky as it was sung by blind beggars at a fair in Kamenka.

In the final *Allegro con fuoco*, a piece in rondo form, there can be no doubt about the origin of the theme with which, after four bars, the piano enters. This is a splendidly vigorous syncopated excerpt from the repository of Ukrainian music. Against it stands a second tune, imaginatively introduced in octaves in the violins and accompanied by the horns. This second tune becomes the climax of the great coda of the concerto, which ends, spectacularly, in a great blaze of colour in major tonality.

On Christmas Eve 1874 Tchaikovsky played his concerto to Nicolas Rubinstein, younger brother of Anton, who had hitherto shown much interest in Tchaikovsky's works. Rubinstein, according to a letter of Tchaikovsky's written three years later, shook the composer by savaging the work: it was unsatisfactory as a whole; it was trivial in matter; the piano part was clumsy, and, indeed, at times, unplayable. In starting thus inauspiciously the concerto, which was revised fifteen years later, was in good company. Schumann's *Phantasie* was at first disregarded by the publisher in Leipzig, and Franck's *Symphonic Variations* met with no success when Liszt performed them at the Festival held in Franck's honour in Paris on 30 January 1887.

It is commonly said that these works are characteristic of their period. This is true. But immediate success more often depends on an ability skilfully to appear up to date, but yet to lag behind the march of progress. Which is why so many estimable musicians fall by the wayside.

Tchaikovsky's second piano concerto, in G major, lacking the expansiveness and the melodic genius of the first, has been overshadowed. Yet when it was first performed in 1882 it was well received. The finest music in this work is in the second movement, where the refined scoring employs solo violin and solo cello in addition to the pianist. In the end the pianist is rather forgotten in this movement so that the concerto element seems to have faded from the composer's mind. The finale, again based on Russian dance tunes, is delightful, humorous, and modest.

The name of Edward Dannreuther will occasionally come to the notice of the amateur musician whose reading strays from the conventional lines. The place he occupied in English musical life in the nineteenth century is best illustrated, however, by the music which he introduced to English audiences. In 1874, at the Crystal Palace, he gave the first English performance of Liszt's second and Grieg's A minor concerto. Two years later he played Tchaikovsky's first concerto.

⁅ EDVARD GRIEG (1843–1907) · Of these works it was Grieg's concerto that appeared most strange and unorthodox to English ears. Three years after its first performance in London Dannreuther gave its second. Then it was assailed by the critic of the *Musical Times*: 'We cannot certainly say that definite themes are wanting in the Concerto, but many of them are uncouth—the first, especially, with the ascent of two augmented fourths in consecutive bars—and they appear thrown together, as if the composer had resolved to use up all the melodies he had jotted down in his sketch-book. Occasionally we have some excellent writing, and the orchestration is exceedingly effective in many parts; but the composition left a sense of weariness upon the audience . . .'

Grieg's concerto was of mixed ancestry. Chopin, Schumann, Liszt, and Norwegian folk music were the dominant strains. From Chopin Grieg learned some part of his figuration; from Schumann, whose concertos played by Clara were one of Grieg's memories of Leipzig, came the general plan; from Liszt, the virtuoso element that distinguishes the great three-part cadenza of the first movement; while the last movement is based on the rhythmic patterns of two country dances.

This concerto, fresh and charmingly done, as in water colours, was agreeably received by two composers whose praise was especially gratifying. On the one hand there was Liszt, whom Grieg visited at Weimar. He played through the work—'with thrilling, magnificent effect, giving vent to the warmest expressions of enthusiasm and singing some of the tunes at the top of his voice as he played'. On the other was Tchaikovsky: 'What charm, what inimitable and rich musical imagery! What warmth and passion in his melodic phrases, what teeming vitality in his harmony, what originality and beauty in the turn of his piquant and ingenious modulations and rhythms, and in all the rest what interest, novelty, and independence.' Above all, Tchaikovsky esteemed 'that rarest of qualities, a perfect simplicity', which in the long run is the source of the concerto's longevity.

The story of the pianoforte concerto in the nineteenth century is the record of Romantic evolution; especially does it show the development of that mainspring of the philosopher-romantics, that art should become universal. For obvious reasons the piano concerto, and to a lesser degree the violin concerto, had the power-ful element of virtuosity with which to delight those whose lives, lacking the spectacular, crave for excitement and colour. The development in the twentieth century of the film industry has given a prolongation of life to the Romantic spirit. Almost every aspect of Romanticism that was reverenced a century, or a cen-tury and a half, ago, is still daily exploited in every cinema. We catch up with the past by degrees. So, while Tchaikovsky, Franck, and Grieg are regarded no more than indulgently by the knowledgeable, those works which have been discussed are (or recently have been) re-popularized. Of the composers within the nineteenth-century tradition, however, it has been Rachmaninov who—through Eileen Joyce, *The Seventh Veil*, and *Brief Encounter* in particular—has most conspicuously conquered the new music lover of the twentieth century. It is, of course, arguable that cinema-goers are not appreciative of music in the highest degree. This may be so, but a disinterested survey of eighteenth- or nineteenth-century opera audiences in Italy or France at least encourages some revision of the standards by which we are apt too exclusively to judge.

⟨ SERGEI RACHMANINOV (1873–1943) · Now Rachmaninov, whose reputation among critics is at present at its nadir, is an eminent example of one born thirty years too late. Rachmaninov, who belonged to a Russian aristocratic family, studied both at St Petersburg and in Moscow, where, as was formerly the case in respect of Tchaikovsky, cosmopolitanism rather than nationalism was idealized. Becoming one of the great pianists of his day, he continued an old virtuoso tradition in cultivating composition as well as performance. His pianoforte works, not surprisingly, are technically perfect. Nor is his skill in orchestration in any way inferior. The fault in Rachmaninov is two-fold: he said virtually nothing that had not been said before, and his style was too patently well-bred.

In all, Rachmaninov wrote four piano concertos. The first, in F sharp minor, was written in 1890–1 when he was still a student, and was issued as his Opus 1; but it was extensively revised and reissued in 1917. The second concerto, in C minor, belongs to the years 1900–1. It was when he was about to commence work on this concerto that Rachmaninov, distressed by the failure of his first symphony and by the attacks of the Russian critics, suffered a severe mental breakdown. Self-confidence gone, Rachmaninov became a patient of a psychologist in Moscow whose treatment was so successful that the composer was able to turn to his project with renewed enthusiasm.

It is the second concerto on which Rachmaninov's reputation in the concert-hall largely depends. And how immediately impressive is the opening: in ten bars the pianist moves solemnly through a succession of rich chords, from *pianissimo* to *fortissimo*. The chords give way to arpeggio figuration (Rachmaninov's style is conspicuous through its ease of arpeggios, which, in fact, became manneristic) and then, *con passione*, a fine, swinging melody appears in the strings [1]. For forty-five bars this melody moves on, richly outlined by the violins, the violas, and the clarinet. The end of the section is marked by some striking variations of colour, as behind the movement of the piano the violins, and then the violas divided into three, melancholically break a descending figure from the previous flow of melody. This passage falls into a heavy atmosphere as the piano chords, supported by dark-toned woodwind, drums, and strings repeat the opening of the melody. The second tune follows, nine bars after [4], and is given by the piano alone. It has been prefaced by a fragment of melody in the violas. By the time the second melody is over one is convinced that originality is not in Rachmaninov, and not all the fine craftsmanship that distinguishes the subsequent development of the melodic material can easily convince one that this is more than facile.

It is, perhaps, a matter of harmony. Imbued with the idea that chords are the effective source of beauty Rachmaninov easily becomes bogged down with clichés. Such it is that the muted strings introduce at the beginning of the slow movement: a glib sequence which goes from C minor to E major, but without anything of the magic quality infused by Dvořák into the similar passage before the slow movement of the *New World* symphony. In E major the piano arpeggios begin, above which, in due course, is a nostalgic melody played by flute and clarinet. Rachmaninov's fluency is marked in this movement, which presses forward, gaining in animation and accumulating decorative passage work in the piano, until a cadenza marks the climax. A return to the opening *adagio* tempo brings the original melody back in the violins. At the end they are surrounded with opulent piano tone and a pattern of arpeggios in the flute and clarinet.

As the popularity of Tchaikovsky's first concerto largely rests on one memorable section, so too does this concerto of Rachmaninov. The 'famous' tune is the second melody of the last movement which appears sixteen bars before [31]. Admirably placed, and magnificently endowed with colour at each subsequent appearance, this is an eminent example of latter-day lyricism. 'Bland', I think, is Edward Sackville-West's term of polite abuse for Rachmaninov, and bland this melody certainly is. At first laid out for viola and oboe, against horns, and then for piano, it draws a line of noble resignation across sixteen bars, the only concession to patent pessimism being in the fifth bar. Then the diatonic contour is modified by the presence of G flat.

Before we arrive at this melody, however, we have made the acquaintance of its fellow, at [28]. The first tune, rhythmic and as near fierceness as Rachmaninov allows himself to approach, is marked by an initial alternation between A flat and G. This melody at first belongs to the piano. And its introduction is another example of the composer's fine craftsmanship. For the third movement begins where the second left off, on a chord of E major. The strings, penetrated by points of woodwind, hint at the rhythm of the forthcoming piano theme and modulate to the appropriate key. The end of the introduction is marked by a cadenza. The concerto concludes in a great burst of tune in C major, wherein the second subject achieves its apotheosis. In the end one is reminded, perhaps, of a passage by Edmund Gosse on Swinburne's *Tristram*: 'In spite of passages of extreme beauty—all of them of the lyrical order—*Tristram* was found to possess the fatal fault of making no progress in the telling of its tale.'

The fatal weakness of the style was revealed accidentally. In 1941 Richard Addinsell was commissioned to write a piece of music for the film *Dangerous Moonlight*—a piece, 'that could be used to become associated in the mind of the audience with Poland, air raids in Warsaw, and whatever the director wanted to suggest'. The result was the *Warsaw Concerto*: Rachmaninov in tabloid form; the perfect background style.

The division of musical history into clear-cut styles and periods is misleading. Just as the classical style outlasted the age which created it and left reactionary composers trailing in its wake, so the Romantic style lingered into the twentieth century. The piano, by nature a romantic instrument, has helped in some part to perpetuate the pattern of mingled wistfulness and grandeur that lie in most of the Romantic concertos.

❮ ERNST VON DOHNÁNYI (*b.* 1877) · The *Symphonic Variations* of César Franck have had one familiar, if not notable, successor in Dohnányi's *Variations on a Nursery Song*. As is Rachmaninov to the Russian tradition so is Dohnányi to the Hungarian, a fine pianist, a skilful if not original composer, and always conscious of the wider fields of music. Thus he ignored the nationalist tradition of Bartók and Kodály, preferring to emulate in an often featureless way the style of Brahms.

Whether the *Variations on a Nursery Song* are humorous or not is a matter of opinion. It is, of course, relatively easy for an accomplished technician to take the melody of 'Baa, baa, black sheep'—or 'Ah, vous dirai-je, Maman' for this is a cosmopolitan tune—and adroitly to dress it from the wardrobe of the modern orchestra. To apply further incongruities through a series of more or less academic variations is also easy. But somehow the joke is a little long-drawn out: one prefers the sort of two-and-a-half minute Hely-Hutchinson 'What shall we do with the drunken sailor' piece (once an engaging detail in the celebrated ITMA programme).

But there is it: Dohnányi gives a tremendous, turgid introduction which, appearing to die in the cellos and basses (which are *pizzicato*) calls for the first big laugh when a *fortissimo* final chord knocks the idea of *perdendosi* out of the ring. Then the theme, demure and be-ribboned, shows against a *pizzicato* background. Eleven variations follow, which provide excellent opportunity for studying the instruments of the orchestra. In the fourth, bassoons and double basses, flutes and piccolo alternate, while the piano chords provide an adequate background to their gambols. In the fifth the melody is given on bells, against a remote *mélange* of piano, harp, and muted string tune. Delightful colouring, of piano and woodwind, distinguishes variation VI. Now come a waltz, a march, a scherzo, a passacaglia, and a chorale. Nor is this all. A fugal finale (which, inevitably, leaves the piano with nothing much to do but chatter) gives a culminating display of academic humour. To make sure that no point is missed the theme is again quoted in the coda, with piano, piccolo, flute, bassoon, and double bassoon chaffing one another. We are brought to earth by a coruscating *molto allegro*, which terminates —as the last firework is exploded—in a piano *glissando*.

A little heavy, maybe, but a relief from the mere respectability of a number of other concertos, ranging from Macdowell to Medtner, which still fill an occasional vacancy in the repertoire.

❲ CO-PARTNERSHIP · The idea that in a solo concerto the solo part should be a display of technical agility, that it should be the dominating feature, is more or less indelible. Assuming that composers write for a public, that the symphony-concert-going public will expect their money's worth from a celebrated performer, and that in time even the most conservative audiences will want something new, it is reasonable that virtuosity should still be a consideration. But from the beginning of this century the piano has been at a disadvantage. Worked at so assiduously during the nineteenth century it must sometimes appear that in conjunction with the orchestra, there is not so very much more that it can say. Also its range of colour has been relatively lessened by the amazing development of virtuosity in orchestral technique. On the whole, the most vivid concertos of recent times have featured instruments other than the piano, which instrument is (for practical purposes) ignored by such significant composers as Strauss, Mahler, and Elgar (who made a half-hearted attempt at a piano concerto), and employed without the greatest enthusiasm by Delius, Vaughan Williams, and Stravinsky.

With the exception of Delius, whose solitary piano concerto in one movement (this changed in 1906 from the three-movement form of 1897) is dismissed with refreshing lack of equivocation by Professor Hutchings as 'drivel', the piano concertos of these composers are, however, of some considerable interest. For they represent attempts, more or less successful, to place the piano in the ensemble as colleague rather than contestant, and to use the medium as a vehicle for the composer's musical ideas rather than for such concessions to performing vanity as he cares to make.

¶ VINCENT D'INDY (1851–1931) · In César Franck we discovered a charming reciprocity as between piano and orchestra, and the piano in the *Symphonic Variations* is, truthfully, a partner in a co-operative enterprise. Vincent d'Indy, Franck's pupil and disciple, was attracted by the possibilities of combining the piano with the orchestra and so composed his *Symphonie sur un chant montagnard français* in 1886. Two other works claim attention for their similar treatment of the piano, Loeffler's *Pagan Poem*, and Falla's *Nights in the Gardens of Spain*.

¶ MANUEL DE FALLA (1876–1946) · In Falla's *Nights in the Gardens of Spain* the style of the piano part is exquisitely shaped by the folk-music character and impressionist sensibility of the music. The tone of the piano, now picking out a quieter figure, and set with the shimmering *glissandi* of the harp, now singing gracefully and modestly and emerging in a 'star inwrought' cadenza of restrained brilliance, is enchantingly indispensable. This is a work of infinite loveliness, indicative of a composer with a rare capacity for seizing beauty in perfected forms. There is nothing imprecise or uncertain about Falla.

❡ BELA BARTÓK (1881-1945) · Nor is there about Bartók, whose stature in contemporary music is such that no work of his can be ignored. As it happens his three piano concertos are not entirely representative, nor so compelling as the violin concerto or the concerto for orchestra. But they are purposeful works.

The importance of the piano in Bartók's development was considerable. In youth, in Budapest, he was regarded as a worthy successor to Dohnányi, under whose influence he came. In his early compositions he was patently indebted to the styles of Liszt (to whose *Dance of Death* he was greatly attached) and of Brahms, who was a fairly regular visitor to Hungary. Many of his earlier works Bartók later disregarded, but not his Opus 1, a Lisztian *Rhapsody* for piano and orchestra. This was completed in 1904. It was about that time that Bartók began his researches, with Kodály, into Hungarian folk music, the character of which infected all his subsequent compositions. But this influence was absorbed into a style which grew as it incorporated elements from practically every tendency in twentieth-century music. In the years after the first world war there was, largely through Stravinsky, a return to basic principles of eighteenth-century music, and to the style of Bach. Thus Bartók's own style is largely direct and uncompromising, sharply melodic and percussively rhythmic.

In the winter of 1927 Bartók paid his first visit to America (where he was later to settle) and among the works he played was his recently completed first piano concerto. In this, one of the first pieces of his mature style, Bartók writes without much regard for the virtuoso and recreates in the outer movements something akin to the texture and movement of a Bach concerto. Much of the material, which is of Magyar origin, is treated contrapuntally. In the slow movement, however, the colour effects of the piano—contrasted chordal groups in high and low registers, expansive arpeggios—show Bartók's affinity with the Impressionist school. Even more is this the case in the second and third concertos. The second concerto is of clearer texture than the first, less obscure in tonality, and of a more 'classical' cast.

At the end of his life Bartók lived, an exile and in great poverty, in America. In executing certain commissions which came to him he attempted more than formerly to accommodate his music to the public ear. In middle life Bartók stood aside, indifferent to praise or censure, and ardently pursued his ambition to synthesize the national Hungarian idiom with current European modes of expression. Resolution often found a severity of utterance that compels respect first and affection (if at all) second. The works of the last period, however, were deliberately designed to be more immediately attractive: so much Bartók felt he owed to his American public.

The third piano concerto was Bartók's last work. It was not quite completed at the time of his death in December 1945, and the final bars were realized from the sketches by his friend Tibor Serly. The first performance of the concerto was by Gyorgy Sando with the Philadelphia Symphony Orchestra, under Eugene Ormandy, on 8 February 1946.

This concerto exemplifies Bartók's magnificent technique as a composer. It is, again, a synthesis of styles. The middle movement, part romantic and part impressionist, is of nineteenth-century stock. In the outer movements, however, the eighteenth century is comprehensively recollected in rigorous counterpoint on the one hand, and in formal orderliness on the other. The Magyar influence is at once apparent in the shape of the first melody of the first movement and in the rhythmic character of the last. The harmonic scheme, typically empirical, is modern in the sense that it is subservient to melody, rhythm, and orchestration and not—as in Rachmaninov or Delius—an end in itself. In common with the majority of eighteenth-century composers Bartók keeps his music effectively and ingeniously moving forward, even if the material out of which it is constructed is not in itself always promising. Thus those who find the 'sewing machine' quality in eighteenth-century music tiresome may rather summarily dismiss the outer movements of this concerto (as also Stravinsky's piano concerto). It is, clearly, a matter of individual taste. For our part we would conclude that any proposition put forward by Bartók is worth consideration, for it is never trivial, and that the outer movements of this concerto justify themselves at least by their acutely intelligent disposition.

It was, I think, in 'Beyle's'[1] life of Haydn that the 'intelligent conversation' of his quartets was pointed out as a signal virtue. The restoration of 'intelligent conversation' to music is one of the encouraging features of contemporary technique. However, if it is 'inspiration' that is required then we must look at the slow movement of Bartók's third concerto. The movement centres on a chorale motiv (bar 6) which is set out five times in block chords on the piano and surrounded by a contrapuntal texture in the strings. In contrast to this plainness there is a nocturnal middle section—*tremolando* strings, piano arpeggios, compressed naturalistic airs from the woodwind, and xylophone giving an impression of distant mysteries—of conspicuous beauty and originality. The last section of the movement is a reprise of the first, piano and strings exchanging roles, with fugitive hints of the interlude and with a climax marked by a stroke on the tam-tam (gong).

❡ MAURICE RAVEL (1875–1937) · Among modern composers there is none whose music is more cultured than Ravel's. Ravel's great contribution to music lies in his perceptiveness, in his perfect fusion of matter and manner. He is, in fact, the great stylist of twentieth-century music. That he should write a piano concerto had been an early ambition, but his two works in this form are in fact among the last things he did. Both were completed in 1931.

At the beginning of 1928 Ravel visited the United States for a concert tour and it was his intention to take with him a Basque Rhapsody (Ravel was of Basque descent on his mother's side) for piano and orchestra. This intention was not fulfilled but during his tour sketches accumulated, from which, in due course, the first and third movements of the G major concerto were made. The principal melody of the first movement, played in the second bar by the piccolo, is obviously of folk-tune provenance—a frivolous derivation from the *branle*, which was a popular dance of the sixteenth century. The first, *allegramente*, and the last,

[1] i.e. Stendhal.

presto, movements have rather less to do with popular dances of the sixteenth century than with the manner of popular music of the present day. The score includes a varied percussion section— tam-tam and wood-block joining the regulars—and the brass and woodwind engage in numerous incidental flippancies not un- familiar in the *palais de danse*. Ravel had a word to say about con- certos which explains the nature of this essay: 'The music of a concerto, in my opinion, should be light-hearted and brilliant, and not aim at profundity or at dramatic effects.'

This being so the G major concerto largely fills the bill. One has, however, a feeling that it does not really come off, that the ideas are factitious, that the whole is shaken out of a rag-bag of technical *tours de force*. The slow movement is variously said to have been inspired by Mozart and by Chopin. If this was the case it must be admitted that neither Mozart nor Chopin would have passed very favourable comment on the melodic content of the movement, however much they might have applauded the expert instrumentation.

The concerto in D minor, for left hand, is in another class. Like many notable works it is the answer to a challenge, having been commissioned by Paul Wittgenstein, a Viennese pianist who lost his right arm in the first world war. The first performance was in Vienna, on 27 November 1931, Wittgenstein being the soloist. In the first place this concerto is a *tour de force*, for with one hand the pianist is required to accomplish more than most can manage with two. Yet it is eminently practicable. The dramatic content of the music, stimulated by the challenge of physical limitations, is as great as anything in Ravel, and the opening passage for double bassoon, against cellos and basses, a remarkable point in orchestral colouring. The concerto is principally based on a sara- bande motiv which stands in contrast to a subsidiary *piu lento* and to a violent finale in jazz idiom.

'Too many classical concertos', said Ravel, 'were composed not so much "for" as "against" the piano.' In the G major concerto he brilliantly vindicates his belief in the central role of the solo part. This with its coverage of the whole keyboard and its cadenzas is a gallant display for the intrepid pianist. No more

effective music could have been contrived by Liszt, the greatness
of whose shadow is once again evident.

❡ SERGEI PROKOFIEV (1891–1953) · The thesis that a concerto
should be light-hearted and brilliant is expounded by no composer
more effectively than by Prokofiev, whose third piano concerto,
in C major, has retained the popularity which it won on its
appearance nearly forty-one years ago. Prokofiev, until his
later and unsuccessful attempts to compose what the Soviet
government thought he ought to write, was exceptional among
twentieth-century composers in having no particular axes to
grind. His best-known works, the 'Classical' symphony, the suite
The Love for Three Oranges, and *Peter and the Wolf*, are clear-cut
in melody and rhythm, but not spectacularly scored, and divert-
ing in their agile changes of tonality. The third piano concerto
(in all, Prokofiev wrote five, four of which have not stayed the
course) has all Prokofiev's characteristic virtues, and thus sounds
a note of lucidity among the mixture of styles to be found in
modern concertos.

Charm is not, perhaps, so highly prized as formerly, and it is
this—note the introductory scoring of each movement—which
dominates the concerto. The first movement is based on two
delicious themes which, apart from an unexpected treatment of
the second in the final section by loud chords on the piano, woodwind, and strings played with the back of the bow (*col legno*), are
developed effortlessly into a genial pattern. It is, however, the
slow movement that principally holds the listener's interest; for
here is a set of variations deserving to be placed among the best
examples of this form. The theme of this *andantino* is a pretty
piece of scoring; first woodwind, then strings, finally a codetta by
flute and clarinet based on the first woodwind phrase. Three
variations follow in which the shape of the theme is evident; the
first marked by piquant harmonics in the piano, the second by
trumpet exhilaration, the third by rhythmic vigour and diversity.
The fourth variation, principally for piano and muted strings, is
—as befits the *andante meditativo* indication—a thoughtful interlude.
The last variation, which leads to a restatement of the theme, is
dominated by great rhythmic energy. The final movement, well

balanced in thematic interest, departs from urbanity in two or three exasperated flings of pianistic temperament, but all thoughts of turbulence are finally dispersed in the glitter of the concluding pages of score. By the side of this work may be set the light-hearted, 'popular', concerto (piano, trumpet, and strings) of Shostakovich, which makes no demands on the listener whatsoever.

⟨ GEORGE GERSHWIN (1898–1937) · In their individual ways both Ravel and Prokofiev affected a popular idiom, but it was George Gershwin who truly inaugurated the era of the 'common man' with the *Rhapsody in Blue*. Quite surprisingly this, too, has had an impressive run for more than thirty years. Newly processed, the latest long-playing records bear testimony to its appeal. Perhaps now it stands a little wanly in the august company it keeps, earnestly endeavouring to justify its first promise as the founder of a dynasty that has never really developed.

⟨ CONSTANT LAMBERT (1905–51) · Numerous composers in America, among them Dana Suesse, Grant Still, and Frederick Jacobi emulated Gershwin, but it may be doubted whether any of them so completely transmuted the jazz idiom of the between-wars years as Constant Lambert, at once the most intellectual and self-critical composer of his generation in England. Lambert, prodigal of his talents, left too little time from literature, conducting, and scholarship to develop to his full stature as composer. But within its limits the *Rio Grande* is the one unassailable masterpiece of its kind. This, a setting of Sacheverell Sitwell's evocative poem, is for chorus, piano solo, and orchestra. Composed in 1929—and the result of some years' consideration of the properties of jazz—the *Rio Grande* won instant acclaim. Spectacular—the sharp light of the poetry is enhanced by the exclusion of woodwind from the orchestra and by the variety within the large percussive section—yet wistful, it satisfied the exotic inclinations of English audiences. Among the solemnities of 1929 the *Rio Grande* stood out for its exhilarating properties. Yet Lambert, as previously in his *Elegiac* Blues, perceived in the jazz idiom the wistfulness that so often lies on the far side of sentimentality. The closing page of *Rio Grande* is, by any standards, an eloquent farewell to a vision of delight.

G

Lambert's music was characterized by a quality formerly rather rare in English music: economy. Thus when he essayed a concerto it was for a chamber ensemble; piano, piccolo, flute, three clarinets, trumpet, trombone, cello, double bass, and percussion. Precise in instrumentation and sharp-edged in rhythm the concerto comprised three movements entitled *Overture*, *Intermede*, and *Finale*, in all of which use was made of jazz characteristics. The work was dedicated to the memory of Peter Warlock, who died in 1930.

Rather outside the main stream of English music, this concerto and the *Rio Grande* bear witness to the empirical nature of national tradition in other respects, and are thus more national than any works of recent years which have subscribed to a more rigorous philosophy.

British composers have, however, a not inconsiderable place in the field of modern concerto. In respect of pianoforte concerto four composers stand out: Walton, Ireland, Bliss, and Rawsthorne.

⁋ WILLIAM WALTON (b. 1902) · Walton's *Sinfonia Concertante*, composed in 1927 but revised in 1943, was based on material intended for a ballet. In many directions it is a work of much interest. Rejecting the conception of the virtuoso concerto the composer incorporated the piano with the orchestra, giving to it hardly more solo passages than any other instrument but, at the same time, making it indispensable. Then, in the matter of form Walton dispensed with the customary methods of recapitulation within each movement, preferring a general summary at the end of the whole work. In thematic content this work is attractive and readily appreciable.

⁋ JOHN IRELAND (b. 1879) · Nor can anyone cavil at the thematic quality of John Ireland's concerto of 1930. This is a romantic work, springing from the pastoral element that characterizes Ireland's not inconsiderable contribution to the pianist's repertoire. In some ways Ireland pursues beauty as determinedly as Rachmaninov, but without any taint of self-pity. Moreover Ireland has a sense of humour, as is evident in the theme (at figure 42) which generates the last movement. This is a brilliant piece of scoring, as may readily be appreciated from following the changes of costume enjoyed by the principal tune. In its own way the concerto unexpectedly owes a little to the jazz fraternity. For at about the time when he was writing it Ireland became acquainted with Jack Payne from whom he learned of the virtues of fibre mutes for brass instruments. Such were specified for the *con sordino* parts of the concerto. It is, however, for the blend of subtlety (note the interrelation of movements by thematic cross-reference) and gaiety that the work is memorable.

❡ ARTHUR BLISS (b. 1891) · Bliss's piano concerto, in the key of B flat major, was commissioned in 1939 for the New York World's Fair. It was dedicated to 'the people of the United States' and played in New York on 10 June 1939, Solomon being the pianist and Sir Adrian Boult the conductor.

Among contemporary concertos this is one of the most rewarding; a regular pageant of sound. Bliss, an extremely accomplished technician, is incapable of indifferent craftsmanship, and his scores are remarkable for their calculated efficiency. One has the impression that Bliss can write adequate music for any occasion—a virtue in a Master of the Queen's Music; whether it is always intrinsically valuable is another matter. It is, however, refreshing to discover a composer who knows his own mind, is content to limit experimentation within well-defined terms of reference, and is sufficiently obliging to meet the audience more than half-way.

In the piano concerto there will be found a fund of agreeable melody, a straightforward diatonic harmonic idiom well seasoned with stimulating dissonance, and a dominating solo part whose behaviour accords with the grand manner. Nothing, for instance, could be more telling than the glitter of the opening octaves in the piano which run into a *marziale* passage of *Pomp and Circumstance* descent and thence to the orchestral exposition of the first subject. We may pick up the strain of brilliance again at figure 6, where an important figure of immense vitality is announced by the brass, in octaves; and again in the large cadenza which, reviewing all the melodic matter of the movement, finishes its extrovert course accompanied by the drums. Much of this has an Elgarian quality (a sketch of a march made by Elgar in the last months of his life, in a 'contemporary' style, comes very near to Bliss), and so have the reflective passages which relieve the *brillante*. Instead, however, of Elgar's stretching sixths and sevenths Bliss exploits the interval of the ninth. Note the haunting tune to which the first subject surrenders: the dreamlike section so gently scored, between figures 14 and 19; and the delicate reflections of the slow movement.

The finale moves slowly away from the contemplative end of the slow movement. From the last echoes of the chord of E major which the strings sounded, the trombones pick up A minor, below which the cellos and basses darkly move. Their tune is translated to the piano which, reaching over several octaves, awakens energy. The cello and basses then deliver a *scherzo* motiv, *molto vivo* and in 6/16 time. The cellos and basses hand over to the violins; they in turn to the violas; then come flutes, and afterwards the drum. Now within the ambit of B flat the piano takes over control and, relentless, pursues the vivacious subject to the end amid a growing accumulation of rhythmic excitement and instrumental colour. If, as is supposed, the British are an athletic race, this is a true expression of that quality.

❲ ALAN RAWSTHORNE (b. 1905) · The final composer in this survey, Alan Rawsthorne, is not unlike Bliss in an inclination to work out his own salvation independently of fashion. Like Bliss, too, Rawsthorne is forthright and lucid. Lancastrian by birth, some of the virtues of his native county may well be detected in his music. On the one hand a pawky humour—as in the *Street Corner Overture*—on the other a perception of beauty amidst the commonplace. Something similar may be found in the art of the Lancashire painter L. S. Lowry. Influenced by Hindemith, Rawsthorne is apparently only interested in musical problems. Programme music is exceptional. His style is characterized by an avoidance of tonal limitations, by a certain uniformity in harmony and rhythm, by a fertile gift for developing melodic formulae through contrapuntal patterns.

Rawsthorne's highly individual style of writing for piano may be seen in his *Bagatelles*, his contrapuntal technique and skill in variation in his early *Theme and Variations* for two violins, his

2 1 1 5

acute appreciation of orchestral values in his *Symphonic Studies*. The first piano concerto, originally scored for piano, strings, and percussion but rescored for its first performance in its present state at a Promenade Concert in 1942 synthesizes the qualities evident in the earlier works. The first movement, a *capriccio*, exploits the toccata figuration as revived from the seventeenth and eighteenth centuries. The second movement, one of Rawsthorne's finest conceptions, continues the baroque manner, for it is a *chaconne*. The third movement is a *tarantella*.

The second concerto, commissioned for the Festival of Britain, was played by Clifford Curzon and the London Symphony orchestra, conducted by Sir Malcolm Sargent, on 17 June 1951. Here, as elsewhere, Rawsthorne departs from the tonal conventions except in one particular. The concerto begins and ends as in F sharp. There are four movements; *allegro piacevole*, of which the *piacevole* element is elucidated in a charming melody set out almost immediately by solo flute above characteristic toccata figuration in the piano part; *allegro molto*, a *scherzo*; *adagio semplice*, with a middle section *poco allegro*; and a final *allegro* which is reminiscent of Walton, the English composer with whom Rawsthorne has the closest affinity.

VI. Concertos for Stringed Instruments

I. VIOLIN

And then with show of skill mechanical,
Marvellous as witchcraft, he would overthrow
That vision with a shower of notes like hail,
Or sudden mixtures of all difficult things
Never yet heard; flashing the sharp tones now,
In downward leaps like swords; now rising fine
Into some utmost tip of minute sound,
From whence he stepped into a higher and higher
On viewless points . . .

❡ NICCOLO PAGANINI (1782–1840) · Such, according to Leigh Hunt, was the peak of the genius of Paganini. And from this mastery flowed the great violin concertos of the nineteenth and twentieth centuries.

Leaving aside the magic of Paganini's personality we are aware from Leigh Hunt of the astounding effect on his contemporaries of his technique. His exploitation of harmonics, of varied tunings, of mixed *arco* and *pizzicato* effects, and his sheer dexterity revolutionized the attitude of the world towards the violin as an instrument. No longer need it take second place to the pianoforte, but could recover the place it held in the age of Corelli and Vivaldi. Paganini's own *capricci* (which exercised the admiration of Schumann, Liszt, Brahms, and Rachmaninov) and concertos are now our sole direct link with him. The two concertos—particularly when played, as they sometimes are, with pianoforte accompaniment—are a disappointment. (It should, however, be said that Paganini's scores as published do not represent exactly what he played; for he was a master of extempore decoration.) The points of virtuosity are still there; but unharnessed to any evident musical purpose.

It is, I suppose, a case of finding what to look for. 'I received', wrote Mrs Hemans, the poetess, 'an eloquent description of a subsequent triumph of his genius. It was a concerto, of a dramatic character, and intended, as I was told, to embody the little tale of a wanderer sinking to sleep in a solitary place at midnight. He is supposed to be visited by a solemn and impressive vision, imagined in music of the most thrilling style. Then, after all his lonely fears and wild fantasies, the day-spring breaks upon him in a triumphant rondo and all is joy and gladness.' Perhaps, even now, there are those for whom Paganini can raise visions of delight.

But there were other qualities, Spohr, the other great violinist of the period, disapproved of Paganini's showmanship but was deeply moved by his incomparable tone. Mendelssohn's father gives another testimonial in a passage from a letter which is equally revealing in relation to his own son:

'Talking of fascination', wrote Abraham from Paris in 1830, 'I was fascinated last night by Taglioni[1]. It is something quite new! You all remember that what most delighted us both in Sontag[2] and Paganini was the placidity, calmness, and composure

---

[1] Marie Taglioni (1804–84), the greatest ballet dancer of the nineteenth century, conspicuous for her blend of classical simplicity and charm.

[2] Henrietta Sontag (1806–54), German soprano.

of their execution. Taglioni's dancing has the same merits: her movements are never rapid, never violent. With perfect self-possession, and without thinking at all about the public, she follows the dictates of her own grace and humour, seeking nothing and finding everything, never making an effort and accomplishing impossibilities.'

❡ MENDELSSOHN · Such criticism is surely apt to Mendelssohn's violin concerto, one of the first great concertos for that instrument of modern times. It is great in that the form is perfectly adapted to the ideas, which themselves are nobly poised between romantic and classic. The first movement of the concerto is marked *allegro molto appassionato*, but the degree of passion is lessened by the succinctness and clarity of the design. It is, of course, on account of its design that the concerto first catches academic approbation. As in the piano concertos the traditional *ritornello* method is abandoned. The violin, high up on the E string, enters after a bar and a half with the first subject; an expressive tune, characterized by the melancholy inclinations of falling intervals. This melody dissolves into more or less brilliant passage work (with arpeggio figuration and double-stoppings—appropriate to the post-Paganini period) which leads towards the relative major key of G. At bar 131 the second subject appears—not intrinsically a compelling melody, but enchantingly delivered by clarinets and flutes above a long, low G, sustained through eight bars by the soloist, who immediately follows the woodwind with the second subject. Both subjects are discussed between the poles of *tranquillo* and *agitato* in the relatively brief development section.

Mendelssohn's views on cadenzas were uncompromising. It was against reason to disturb the flow of a work simply to titillate the ear. However, the man-of-the-world part of his character informed him that a concerto entirely cadenza-less was no genuine concerto. So, in this instance, the cadenza was written, but incorporated as a necessary part of the whole. It succeeds the development and prefaces the recapitulation, into which it tumbles happily, as violins, flute, and oboe, *pianissimo*, introduce again the first subject. Despite the appearance of the second subject in E major the end part of the movement is resolute in minor tonality and the concluding *presto* and *sempre piu presto* move under grey skies. Clearly as the solo part cuts incisively into the score this is very much a concerto for, and not against, the violin.

The first movement runs on into the second. And at this point Mendelssohn goes as near mystery as ever he allowed himself. A solitary bassoon sustains one note from the first movement, then resolves it upwards by a semitone to the tonic of the *andante*, which is in C major. Above the bassoon comes the flute, and below the violas. Violins and cellos follow, and the accompaniment figure runs for four bars before the solo part enters with a memorable melody. Elegant, slenderly wistful, but nearly commonplace, this *cantilena* typifies the man and his environment. Sensibility was highly regarded at the Gewandhaus concerts in Leipzig and this is the prevailing quality. The middle part of this ternary piece hints again at distant mysteries in the peremptory intermissions from the brass, the more urgent rhythm, the movement of the solo part; but it is all kept well within the bounds of reason.

Throughout the concerto one is aware of a transparency in the orchestration. If anyone had asked Mendelssohn why he had written the work he might well have used the classic answer of John Crome to one who asked him why he had painted 'Mousehold Heath': 'for air and space'. The *allegro molto vivace*, prefaced by an introductory *allegretto non troppo*, is an exquisite study of sunshine. Occasionally one should take the ear off the brilliant solo part and consider the delicate interplay of woodwind and strings. Within this concerto there is room for the soloist, given the necessary technique to work out his own salvation. It is not so heavily impressed with the composer's emotions that the player cannot, up to a point, mould it with his own personality. Thus it retains its first popularity.

Mendelssohn had this concerto in mind for half a dozen years. Thus he gave more thought to it than to his piano concertos. With regard to the solo part he was advised throughout by Ferdinand David, for whom it was written and by whom it was first performed at the Gewandhaus on 13 March 1845.

David resembled Mendelssohn in many ways. He was an intellectual, interested in a wide range of subjects, and with wide musical sympathies that led him to crusade vigorously for a revival of the violin sonatas of the eighteenth century. He held no brief for any particular method either in playing or composition. Thus, as violinist he was able to synthesize the breadth and dignity of Spohr—his master—with the technique and verve of Paganini; but his virtuoso talent was ever subordinate to the requirements of the music. David was also a great teacher, his most brilliant pupil being Joachim.

❲ SCHUMANN · Besides the great concerto of Brahms two other works are specially associated with Joachim: the concertos of Schumann and Dvořák. It would be difficult to find two more contrasted works. Schumann's concerto was a late work, moving between the storm and stress of the opening of the first movement and the sense of resignation that marks the slow movement. Written in the autumn of 1853, when Joachim was a constant visitor with Brahms to the Schumanns in Düsseldorf, the violin concerto has much in common with the violin sonatas, which, however, are works of finer quality. The concerto was never finally revised by the composer and, after Clara Schumann and Joachim had decided against its publication, only issued in 1937.

❲ ANTONIN DVOŘÁK (1841–1904) · Dvořák's concerto for violin does not compare with that for cello, but it is a delightful and characteristic work. In 1878 Joachim, much attracted by Dvořák's sextet in A major (Opus 48) and quartet in E flat (Opus 51), asked that he should write a violin concerto. Having completed a provisional score Dvořák sent it to Joachim and included his suggestions in a revised score. The concerto was played for the first time in Prague in 1883.

Dvořák, like Sibelius, Elgar, and Bloch, was a violinist himself, and his understanding of the instrument is apparent when the violin concerto is compared with the earlier, unsuccessful piano concerto (Opus 33). Lacking balance—the first movement being too short and the second too long—the violin concerto is less effective than the cello concerto, but extraordinarily full of delicious, unmistakably Bohemian ideas. The slow movement is a long rhapsody in which the violin is rarely rested; the finale an infectious Slavonic dance, full of cheerful country life.

⁋ TCHAIKOVSKY · Of the same period as Dvořák's concerto is that of Tchaikovsky, which had its first performance in Vienna in 1879. Tchaikovsky's interest in violin music was through Leopold Auer, a pupil of Joachim, who was court violinist and professor of the violin at St Petersburg. It was, however, not Auer but Brodsky (later a powerful influence on English violin playing, through his long residence in Manchester) who first played the concerto.

Vienna was the wrong place; for a year previously Brahms's violin concerto had been received as the last word by the critics, headed by Hanslick. Tchaikovsky's concerto for him was altogether too effusive. It is the last movement which stands out by reason of melodic ebullience, as Russian as anything that Tchaikovsky wrote. There are three striking themes: the first, impetuous in Cossack rhythm; the second, *poco meno mosso*, drawn at first over a drone bass; and the third divided at the outset between oboe and clarinet. It is, however, the first of the themes which conditions the general character of the whole movement.

In the first movement Tchaikovsky has left in enough of those passages which Auer declared to be unplayable; notably the cadenza which is almost beyond the limits of probability. Curiously, however, the melodic content of the movement is relatively simple, so that the principal melodies—see bars 28 and 69—are of genial, lyric quality. The dramatics are not in the themes but impressed on them by the virtuoso properties of the instrument, and the orchestra. One of the features of this concerto is the splendour of the orchestral score. To take two points of colour in the first movement: study the passage from bar 69 to bar 127. The violin modestly and expressively begins the second subject by singing above a quiet landscape of string tone. At bar 81 the accompaniment, warmed by the tone of horns, is irradiated by the clarinet. The woodwind enter in chorus and the soloist rises to a high pitch of excitement. The part becomes more virtuosic. The background changes again as behind rapid triplets there are short, *pianissimo* chords in the woodwind alone. This accompaniment figure is later shared with the strings. At bar 119 a sequence of trills in the solo part, and a flight of arpeggios mark the end of the first section of the movement. The woodwind increase their contribution and a blazing *crescendo*, against the most widely flung figure from the violin so far heard, leads to the development section. Here a melody derived from the first subject stands out in fine military full dress uniform.

The slow movement, entitled *canzonetta*, represents second thoughts. Tchaikovsky was dissatisfied with his first attempt, though not so much so as to destroy it. The *Meditation*, the first of the three pieces of Opus 42, is the original slow movement. The *canzonetta* is set within Tchaikovsky's frequent melancholic temper. Beautifully coloured, it means either something or nothing: one is moved or not moved. The craftsmanship, which is considerable, is largely irrelevant to the matter of appreciation. At the same time it is worth looking for the part played by the clarinet which, from time to time, exerts an influence beyond the notes it has to produce: its tone colour affects the general atmosphere.

⁅ MAX BRUCH (1838-1920) · 'In music', wrote Bernard Shaw in 1892, 'there is still a general impression that the form makes the composer, and not the composer the form. Bruch's Scottish fantasia is much better than his concertos; but it is on the strength of his concertos that he is regarded as a sort of contemporary old master.'

By some curious quirk of fortune Bruch still hangs on to the tail of classical respectability on the strength of his first violin concerto in G minor. At the beginning of this work Bruch does, indeed, essay novelty in the preludial dialogue between violin and orchestra; but the thematic material of the work and its general behaviour does not dispose one towards classing the composer as an inspired artist. A comfortable concerto to play, giving illusions of the dramatic and the monumental, violinists have always looked at it with affection and the rest of us with respect because it comes out of performance better than it goes in.

⁅ PABLO SARASATE (1844–1903) · The form of the first movement of Bruch's concerto is a reminder that in his hey-day his reputation depended rather more on his choral works than his orchestral; the *Scottish Fantasia*, written for Sarasate, of his interest in folk music. Fantasias and romances for violin and orchestra were very much part of the nineteenth-century pattern, and no-one in the latter part of the century had a finer fantasia-style of performance than Sarasate.

This great Spanish violinist was a travelling virtuoso of the regular order. France—he was trained at the Paris Conservatoire —Portugal, Norway, America, England: it mattered not where he went or what he played, his rhetorical method of playing and his amazing dexterity held audiences spellbound. The highlight of his performances was his own arrangements of Spanish dances. Apart from such pieces of his as are in the repertoire of violinists his principal monument is Lalo's inspiriting *Symphonie Espagnole*. Previously Lalo had written a more authentic concerto (in F major) for Sarasate; but his ear for colour found happier opportunities in programme rather than in abstract music. Besides the *Symphonie espagnole*, which was written in 1875, Lalo composed a *Fantaisie norvégienne* and a *Concerto russe* for violin and orchestra.

⁅ JEAN SIBELIUS (b. 1865) · The elements that were the basis of nineteenth-century music—classical, romantic, and national— all meet in the music of Sibelius and are welded into an indissoluble whole. Sibelius's violin concerto in D minor was written in 1903, a year after the second symphony, with which it has certain affinities. This is an unjustly neglected concerto, largely it would seem because the solo part, although of great difficulty, does not sound as nearly impossible as most virtuosi require. The first movement is characteristically unconventional, but convincing. There are three, instead of two, groups of melodies: in D minor, B flat major, and B flat minor. These, with attendant motivs, form an exposition of mingled austerity and ferocity. The cadenza, based on the first melody, appears midway in this movement, and the development and recapitulation are blended into one final section, at the end of which brief reference is made to the cadenza. The second movement, *adagio di molto*, delivers a lyrical melody of great beauty, which comes first from the solo violin and then from the orchestra. The last movement, an energetic study in rhythms that are more perplexing to eye than to ear, is a rondo of genial, Karelian character.

In addition to the concerto, Sibelius wrote, in 1903, two *Serenades*, and in 1917, six *Humoresques* for violin and orchestra, which are excellent examples of his skill in disposing of unusual groups of instruments.

❡ MORE VIRTUOSI · At the turn of the century the violin was very much in the ascendant. One virtuoso player after another toured Europe and America. Ondříček, the Czech who had first played Dvořák's concerto; Ysaÿe, the Belgian, who was the teacher of Bloch; Kubelik, also Czech, the first of the notable pupils of Ottokar Sevčik, whose devotion to the science of violin playing was phenomenal, and whose influence on style prodigious; and Fritz Kreisler were the principal celebrities. To a greater or lesser degree all these virtuosi were composers, Kubelik being, perhaps, most prominent in this respect. Among his works were six violin concertos, which, admirably designed to display his own technique, were competent if not exceptional. It was, however, Kreisler who stimulated the composition of a great work.

As early as 1904 Kreisler suggested that if the rumour that Elgar had written a concerto was true he would be delighted to play it. Elgar, in fact, had made sketches for such a concerto but had never followed them up. However, as with many other projects, he let the idea take shape in his mind and in 1909, still with Kreisler in view, he commenced his violin concerto. It was ready for performance at a Philharmonic Concert on 10 November 1910, where it was played by Kreisler, to whom it is dedicated.

❡ EDWARD ELGAR (1857–1934) · This concerto is a magnificent vindication of Shaw's thesis that a composer should make musical form. Elgar, whose early training was from the standard textbooks, never strayed unduly far from the main architectural principles of classical style. In the violin concerto he went back to the introductory exposition of themes by the orchestra. Thus it is not until the seventieth bar that the soloist enters. In the introduction there is a wealth of melodic invention, the main points of which are to be picked up at bars 1, 5, 9, 15, 31, and 46.

Such fragments of tune found their way into his sketch books as soon as they occurred to him. In this we can see something of ourselves; for most of us with any pretensions to being musical can invent promising *incipits* to tunes. It is in the subsequent treatment that the difference between musical aptitude and musical genius becomes apparent. It will be noticed that in Elgar's first movement these themes appear as inevitable, not only because of their progression towards imaginative climaxes but also because of their scoring.

When the solo violin appears—after an invitatory repetition of the first two bars of the concerto—it deals with the themes which have already been expressed according to its own fancy. The traditional plan of development and recapitulation is followed, but the plan is subordinate to the emotional conviction that is the distinguishing mark of the work.

Like Schumann, whom he resembled in many ways, the best of Elgar is often to be found in his slow movements. Here is a ruminative movement, in the distant key of B flat major, in which the central decorative flourishes of the soloist add radiance to the score. Sensitive always to natural beauty, Elgar here—in music written under Italian skies—achieves something akin to the vivid tenderness of Perugino. In the brilliant final movement the celebrated feature is the cadenza, accompanied by a *pizzicato tremolando* by the strings. 'You will like the cadenza which is a novel plan I think', wrote Elgar to his friend Frank Schuster, '—accompanied very softly by a few insts. and—it comes at the end of the last movement—it surely thinks over the 1st movement.' It is in the same letter that Elgar summarizes the *meaning* of the work: 'This Concerto is *full* of romantic feeling—I would have been a philanthropist if I had been a rich man—I *know* the feeling is human and right—vainglory!'

Always enigmatic, Elgar prefaced the violin concerto with a Spanish quotation which he translated: 'Here, or more emphatically *in here* is enshrined or simply enclosed—burial is perhaps too definite—*the soul of* . . .?' A good deal of speculation has attached to this interrogation. There is no definite answer, nor, I think, was there ever meant to be. Elgar, I think, believed in an interfusion of souls in love and friendship so that the capacity of the soul is infinite.

Until the advent of Elgar it was generally understood that such talent as English composers might possess was embedded in choral music. Since Elgar, however, the English contribution to music has been more conspicuous through instrumental channels. Six or seven violin concertos, at least, have made their mark. In chronological order those of Delius, Vaughan Williams, Bax, Walton, Moeran, Rawsthorne, and Bliss stand out as possessing some special interest. The English pastoral style, bounded on the one side by folk song and on the other by an unsensational brand of impressionism, is not always regarded with favour. True, it is not world-beating stuff, but those who have an eye for Cotman and de Wint, not to mention the greater East Anglians, may well have an ear for the violin concertos of Delius, Bax, and Moeran.

❡ FREDERICK DELIUS (1862–1934) AND ARNOLD BAX (1883–1953) · That of Delius, written for Albert Sammons in 1906, is a rhapsody in fact—one movement with three sections. It disguises its difficulties, is memorable for Brigg Fair tunefulness, for characteristically succulent harmonics, and for undulating instrumental backgrounds in which the harp and woodwind come and go. In Bax's concerto of 1937 there is plenty of open-air music—in the ballad theme which is at the centre of the first movement, in the character both of melody and of orchestration of the *adagio*, and in the opening theme of the final *allegro*. Bax, however, moulds his material far more effectively than Delius, and since the instrumentation of this concerto is free from the thickness which mars much of Bax's work, this is in consequence in true concerto style.

❡ E. J. MOERAN (1894–1950) · In Moeran there are affinities with Bax, as also with Vaughan Williams. A collector of folk song and deeply affected by the scenery of Norfolk and the west coast of Ireland, Moeran was essentially a Romantic composer. The violin concerto, in D major, is a thoroughly representative work; straightforward, diatonic, sometimes modal melodies, set in a colourful harmonic and orchestral framework, with a regard for beauty and a respect for humour, provide the index to a familiar countryside. At the back of the music is the sense of the Wordsworthian immanent spirit. So the order of the movements is unusual—*allegro moderato, rondo,* and, finally, *lento.* The end is in contemplation.

⟨ VAUGHAN WILLIAMS (b. 1872) · Vaughan Williams has on the one side his *Lark Ascending,* a pastoral *concertino* in miniature, and on the other the *Concerto Accademico.* The latter was first performed by Jelly d'Aranyi, Joachim's great-niece, in 1925. This plain, home-spun piece shows Vaughan Williams digging not unprofitably among the tombs of the eighteenth century.

⟨ WALTON · All these works, however, are of local significance. It was left to Walton to break into the export market with the violin concerto which he wrote for Heifetz, and which was first played by him on 7 December 1939, at Cleveland, Ohio. In this work Walton displays a technical mastery unrivalled by any other English composer in the same field. The solo part, edited by Heifetz, is of the greatest difficulty, but virtuosity never obtrudes. One of the last of Walton's compositions in definite tonality— the key is B minor—it is not without its romantic proclivities. These are most obvious in the ingenious second movement, a scherzo-trio, entitled *Presto capriccioso alla napoletana,* the latter qualification referring to the waltz-like theme. In this movement is the climax of violin virtuosity. The first movement, spacious yet restrained at the outset, is of great nervous vitality, extending from the reflective quality of the first violin theme to the detailed comment of the development section. In the last movement, with a 'Crown Imperial' conclusion, are more outspoken, more extrovert, more readily appreciable ideas. Not the least impressive feature of the movement is the accompanied cadenza. No doubt this is music which, as is said, grows on one. It should be remembered that it is cut out of hard material, but this does not preclude beauty. After all, some of the best of English sculpture is in alabaster.

⟨ RAWSTHORNE · Alan Rawsthorne's violin concerto, first played by Theo Olaf and the Hallé Orchestra, conducted by Barbirolli, at the Cheltenham Festival of 1948, shows again that

H

affinity of style with Walton which is evident in the second piano concerto. This is not surprising, for the violin concerto is dedicated to Walton. This, the most ambitious of Rawsthorne's concertos, is more highly organized and less rhapsodic than those for piano. There are two movements, flexibly developed in a manner somewhat reminiscent of Schumann. Throughout the first movement Rawsthorne, like Vaughan Williams in the sixth symphony, is fascinated by the relationship between major and minor thirds. Thus we follow the recitative introduction, the pensive opening of the succeeding *andante con moto*, *poco temperamente*, the *piu mosso*, and discover that all the melodic material stems from a common root. But within the limits thus set there is considerable development in harmonic and instrumental colour as also in the range of the solo part. This reaches a climax in a cadenza, after which the movement ends with a more or less formal recapitulation. The coda is as the recitative introduction. The final movement, a cross between rondo and variations, is remarkable for the vitality with which the motiv set out at letter [A] is developed contrapuntally. The solo part of this work is rather less than virtuoso, being conceived in relation to context, and frequently it is associated with other instruments, thus producing a *concertino* effect. If lucidity is the characteristic of the disposition of melodic material, so also it marks the scoring. If one instrument will suffice then one is used. With economy comes strength and the instrumental colours are brightened by extensive edging by percussion.

⟨ BLISS · Sir Arthur Bliss's concerto, commissioned by the B.B.C. and first performed by Campoli and the B.B.C. Symphony Orchestra in 1955, is outwardly adventurous—the solo part being spectacular in the extreme but after a familiar order—but intrinsically conservative. The opening movement is in more or less regular sonata form; the second movement a scherzo partly inspired by Berlioz's *Queen Mab*; and the finale an introduction, theme, and variations, and *allegro deciso* (*in modo zingaro*). Bliss notes of the last movement that 'the gipsy feeling is a tribute to my soloist's temperament'. In the *Musical Times* (June 1955) he indicates the extent to which he was influenced by Campoli.

'I began rehearsing the first two movements . . . while deeply considering the third. I let myself be swayed by the style of playing of my chosen soloist, just as a playwright might be influenced by a great actor in his leading role. Campoli and I have had many rehearsals together. He has been tireless in discussing the work— almost bar by bar—in suggesting how difficult and awkward passages can be made more amenable, and in giving me, by his masterly playing, stimulation to further work.' So Elgar (who went through every bar of his concerto with W. H. Reed as well as Kreisler), Tchaikovsky, Brahms, Mendelssohn, and many others might have written of their partners. So, up to a point, are we enabled to appreciate some aspect of concerto music through knowledge of the style of the playing of the great performer.

❡ BARTÓK · Since the indisputably notable concertos form a highly select body we should leave the cheerful corpus of contemporary English concertos (whose significance will be clearer in the course of the next few years) and turn aside to that which has been reckoned as possibly the greatest work of the past quarter-century: Bartók's concerto, written in Budapest in 1937–8 for the Hungarian violinist Zoltán Székely.

It is often adduced that 'modern' music is deficient in melody. To some extent this is true, if what we look for in melody is a patently singable quality: but, as in Rawsthorne, instruments as well as voices can be the source of melody and in this case the structure of melody will necessarily be of a different order. Now great music is that which, aware of the general tendencies of style, favours none to the exclusion of others. Bartók's concerto has a synoptic view. It has classical proportions, is unashamedly national in many particulars, acknowledges the 'twelve note' schematism of Schoenberg and his considerable following, is dramatic and lyrical by turns, and is yet acceptable to the ear at a first hearing. The immediate source of gratification to the listener lies in the long melodic lines.

The first movement introduces one such in the first subject, a Magyar-type tune, which is introduced by harp chords and *pizzicato* strings. The influence of this melody is strong throughout the movement. We may note its expansion into counterpoint at [43], and at [179]; its inversion at [194] against a setting of high strings, harp and celesta; its reprise at [213]; its imaginative colouring in the coda; and we may feel the dynamic undercurrent of its rhythm generally. This binding quality is enhanced by the contrasting character of the subsidiary themes; of the busy semi-quaver motiv first stated at [22]; and of the ethereal second subject at [73].

Here, marked *calmo* and set against a pulsating figure in the lower strings, shines a theme of precisely twelve notes. These twelve notes are restated, though not in the same order, by the strings. This theme, following the Schoenbergian technique up to the first stage at least, comprises all the notes within the octave. But Bartók handles the material with imagination. This theme is the ideal foil to the more personal nature of the previous material. It is after this section that the one problematic moment of the music occurs. At [92] woodwind and strings skirmish in F minor against the brass which firmly hold to D major. Why? The answers to this question are various. Ingenuously one commentator rides away from the incident which is described as a climax. Another reads into it a gesture of defiance against the Schoenbergians. Yet another finds the second subject itself satirical. This will certainly not do, for the passage itself is possessed of a visionary quality—and here, perhaps, we have the key to the problem. A vision of beauty may last for no more than a moment. Then it is shattered. So here. Bartók (the 'twelve note' basis is neither here nor there) feels himself to have attained something ordinarily inaccessible. Suddenly the faculty vanishes and a demonic power asserts itself. Something similar occurs in the *intermezzo interrotto* in the *Concerto for Orchestra*.

The slow movement of the concerto is a theme with six variations. The theme again reflects folk music in rhythmic and melodic inflections, and the treatment of the solo instrument is redolent of gipsy music. The light scoring of the movement deserves close attention, for extraordinarily original colouring evolves from the simplest combinations. Note the accompaniment of solo violin at the beginning of the first variation by double bass and timpani, the sheen of high woodwind, high strings, and harp runs in the second variation, the mysterious background of low strings and clarinet in the fourth, the delicate and fanciful glitter of the fifth, the percussive pointing of the string canon in the sixth. In each case the orchestration is part of the music from the beginning.

The third movement, robust and classically ordered, is entirely complementary to the first. It will in fact be seen that the two principal themes, the first of which is stated by the violin after four rumbustious bars of introduction and the other, *quasi lento*, after [126], are variants of the two subjects of the first movement.

In every case in this work the principal themes are first announced by the soloist, whose supremacy is never in doubt.

⟦ ALBAN BERG (1885–1935) · A year before Bartók set to work on his violin concerto one by the Austrian composer Alban Berg was performed at Barcelona. This was Berg's last work, perhaps his greatest, certainly his most poignant. For some time before he began this composition Louis Krasner, the American violinist who made the work very much his own, urged Berg to write a concerto for him. It was the death of a young friend—Manon Gropius—which finally gave him the inspiration he required. The expressive quality of the violin has affected mystically poets and musicians alike. The violin can, it often seems, carry human feeling into infinite reaches. Berg's concerto is all compassion, anguish, acceptance of fate. That it is composed according to the 'twelve note' system is less important than that it is exquisitely moving. The work is in two parts, each part comprising two movements. Part I consists of a dream-like *andante* and an *allegretto* of which the two trios catch local colour in waltz and *ländler* rhythm. Part II contrasts a catastrophic *allegro* with an *adagio*. The *adagio* is based on the chorale 'Es ist genug' from Bach's church cantata, No. 60, *O Ewigkeit, du Donnerwort*. Finely disciplined, for Berg composed with mathematical precision, the concerto is nonetheless a unique extension of Romantic impulse. For the essence of the music lies in its exposition of feeling and it is the *in memoriam* quality which remains longest in mind. Berg inscribed his concerto 'To the Memory of an Angel', whose spiritual nature is defined in the white beauty of the coda.

II. VIOLA

❡ HECTOR BERLIOZ (1803–1869) · The suggestion that the viola might be taken seriously as a solo instrument came from Paganini. In the winter of 1833 he was in Paris and, after hearing the *Symphonie Fantastique* at the Conservatoire, he recognized in Berlioz a composer after his own heart. Stimulated by Berlioz's striking powers of orchestration he proposed that he should write for him a work for viola. Paganini possessed an instrument by Stradivari, but as virtually no music existed for viola (and as he was not disposed to write any) he was unable to demonstrate its beauty. Berlioz, although no lover of the contemporary style of virtuoso music, undertook to write a work with, at any rate, a prominent part for viola. Sketches accumulated, therefore, towards a fantasy—for chorus, orchestra, and solo viola—to be entitled *Les Derniers Instans de Marie Stuart*. A melancholic send-off for the viola; and so Paganini thought. In any case, he protested, there was not enough for the viola to play, and what there was was quite unbrilliant. Berlioz thereupon declared himself unable to comply with Paganini's request.

But the potentialities of the tone of the viola continued to absorb his interest. The viola, surely, had some contribution to make to music of the Romantic era. It could, perhaps, represent the dreamer. Byron's *Childe Harold*, for example. Byron's poem, completed in 1818, was much in Berlioz's mind, not only because of its congenial character but also because Berlioz himself had spent part of 1831 and 1832 in Italy. The result was the symphony *Harold in Italy* which, begun immediately after the abortive attempt on *Les Derniers Instans de Marie Stuart*, was completed by the summer of 1834.

Harold in Italy was given a successful first performance in November, but its success was due more to the general narrative and illustrative quality of the work than to any outstanding interest in the viola part. But the viola serves to impress on the work the character of its hero, and thus to expand the system of the *idée fixe* as previously shown in the *Symphonie Fantastique*. The four movements of *Harold in Italy* are: *Harold aux montagnes*; *Scènes de mélancolie, de bonheur et de joie*; *Marche de pélerins*, a more pictorial piece than the slow movement of Mendelssohn's *Italian Symphony* which partly suggested it; *Sérénade d'un montagnard des Abruzzes à sa maîtresse*, a pastoral episode; and *Orgie de brigands*. Midway between opera and symphony, *Harold in Italy* deserves more performances than it receives. But the viola is, even now, not a fashionable instrument.

After *Harold in Italy* it was nearly a hundred years before the viola showed itself again with any moderate degree of prominence. Strauss wrote a character part, as for Sancho Panza, in *Don Quixote*, and Elgar an appealing movement ('Ysobel') in the *Enigma Variations*; but it was not until the twentieth century that such players appeared as would make it worth a composer's while to compose extensively for the instrument.

⟦ LIONEL TERTIS (b. 1876) · The pioneer of the modern viola school was Lionel Tertis, who was persuaded to the viola by Sir Alexander Mackenzie, Principal of the Royal Academy of Music when Tertis was a student there. Tertis rapidly became known as the leading exponent of the instrument and toured extensively in Europe and America. There being little other than arrangements to play Tertis encouraged those of his friends who were composers to consider his needs. The earliest concerto specially written for him was that by John McEwen, the Scottish composer, and, later, Mackenzie's successor at the Royal Academy in 1901. Although a number of composers, including Bax (*Phantasy* for viola and orchestra, 1920), wrote slender works for the medium, progress was slow and it was not until 1929, when Walton's concerto was performed, that a work of sufficient significance to compare with similar works for piano or violin was heard.

⟦ WALTON AND PAUL HINDEMITH (b. 1895) · Walton's concerto was played for the first time at a Promenade Concert, and the soloist was Paul Hindemith, who now claims his own place in this section. Hindemith too was (and still is) a fine viola player, having been a member of the Amar Quartet. Among Hindemith's works the viola appears prominently. There are three sonatas

with piano, two unaccompanied sonatas, a number of chamber
works in which the instrument is conspicuous, and *Kammermusik
No. 5*—a concerto after the eighteenth-century manner for solo
viola and chamber orchestra. This, written in 1927, was one of a
group of pieces in which Hindemith's rigorous linear technique
attracted considerable attention. A later work, *Der Schwanendreher*
(1935), is of more immediately congenial quality. It is, in effect,
a folk song suite (the title is from the song on which the variations
of the last movement are based) for viola and orchestra. 'A min-
strel', the composer noted on his score, 'joining a merry company, displays what he has brought back from foreign lands:
songs serious and gay, and finally a dance piece—like a true
musician he expands and embellishes the melodies, preluding
and improvising according to his fancy and ability. This mediaeval
scene was the inspiration of the composition.' This four-movement work—remarkable for the exclusion of orchestral violins
and violas—was first performed by Hindemith himself with the
Concertgebouw Orchestra of Amsterdam.

Walton's concerto may well remain as one of the most impressive of his works. Already it is something of a classic, and
not solely on account of the lack of competition in this particular
field. It is superbly written and fully exposes the variety within
the tonal range of the viola. Reflectiveness occurred to Berlioz
as a particular quality of the viola, and this is the mood of Walton's first movement. The first is in fact the slow movement of the
concerto, but marked by dramatic development of the two principal themes, the first, of a pastoral character, being almost immediately announced by the viola, the second at [4]. In this
concerto one is aware of the singing quality of an instrumental as
distinct from a vocal line. The intervals of the ninth, the rhythmic
disposition of notes, the phrasing all spring from an instrumental
source. It is the witty, complex rhythm of the second movement
(c.f. *Portsmouth Point*) that caused, I remember, some consterna-
tion in Worcester Cathedral when the concerto was first heard
at a Three Choirs Festival a quarter of a century ago. It was as
though gargoyles had taken musical shape. This third movement,
allegro moderato, leads from the purposeful comedy of the *scherzo*

by way of a metamorphosis of the principal theme of the *scherzo* (now given to bassoon), to a lyrical second subject, in which a sequence of sixths is a feature, four bars after [40]. From here the music grows more majestic, more contrapuntal. At the end the viola quotes the first subject of the first movement, and against it is set in the strings the melody with which the finale commences. For those of a ruminative disposition Edmund Rubbra's viola concerto, dedicated to William Primrose, is recommended as a charming introduction to this composer's work. Not, perhaps, a piece that will endure for ever, this concerto, standing aside from the hurly-burly of modernity, carries a plain, lyrical quality typical of Rubbra and apt to this medium.

❦ MISCELLANEOUS PIECES · Apart from concertos by Bartók (completed from Bartók's sketches by Tibor Serly) and Quincy Porter, which are rarely played, the rest of the story of the viola as solo instrument in the concert hall is in more or less slender works in suite or fantasy form. The most outstanding work in this group is Bloch's Suite for viola and orchestra (also available for viola and piano), which shows fantastic colour sense and characteristically passionate feeling. Otherwise there are Vaughan Williams's charming and modest set of pieces written for Tertis in 1934 and a fine *Elegy* by Herbert Howells. Running through all is the air of seriousness which Berlioz recognized, and which, it seems, is inescapable.

III. CELLO

❦ DVOŘÁK · 'Why on earth didn't I know that one could write a violoncello concerto like this? If I had only known, I would have written one long ago!' So said Brahms when, in 1895, he first read through the score of Dvořák's concerto in B minor. The wonder of this work is its unflagging melodic exuberance. There was hardly another composer—always excepting Schubert —whose capacity for tune-making was richer than Dvořák's, and in the cello concerto the faculty is at its height.

At the first time of hearing it is enough, perhaps, to relax within the melodic flow; noting, at the same time, that the quality of orchestration is almost equally absorbing. But there is more to it than this: the work carries the mark of inevitability that indicates fine design.

The first movement, indeed, is something of a structural masterpiece. It commences, according to classical precedent, with an orchestral exposition of the two principal themes. Of these the first is introduced at once by the clarinets—joined after two bars by the bassoons. Then the violins, coloured by oboe tone, take over and, with increasing passion, lead to a *grandioso* statement by full orchestra. This accomplished, some gracefully derivative matter, countrified by ornamentation in the woodwind, prepares the way for the entry of the horns at bar 66. Here is the second principal theme. The clarinets at first, and now the horn, herald the solo cello by marking out the area of pitch in which the main interest of this concerto must lie.

The cello apparently has a natural tendency to rhapsodize and so when it is given the first subject (now set off with a major instead of a minor third) the score is marked *quasi improvisando*.

But the improvisatory element must be controlled, for not the least part of the attraction of this section lies in the interplay of cello and woodwind tune. Indeed the notable role of the woodwind department is conspicuous throughout the whole work. This is practical commonsense: for the cello stands out against woodwind with more clarity than against brass.

The cello having dealt with the exposition of the two themes a rhapsodic interlude (wherein new themes freely come and go) ensues: but the rhapsodic is subdued, at bar 191, when the first theme, again *grandioso*, asserts mastery in the full orchestra. But this tune has another facet. So, at bar 224, the cello, which for some time has been silent, introduces it plangently, in the key of A flat minor—a long way from home—and flute (for which Dvořák had great affection) and oboe comment on the new turn of events. But a quickening *tempo*, rising energy, and a display of double-stopping by the cello which culminates in the sweep of an ascendant, chromatic scale lead to more positive thoughts. At bar 267 the recapitulation begins. But it is the second subject which now comes first; the first subject maintaining its right to supremacy by insisting on the last word. And so, ennobled by the brass, it dominates the conclusion.

The central *adagio* is at once all innocence; an ingenuous melody for the clarinet, accompanied by oboes and bassoons, setting it on its way. Before long, and unobtrusively picking up the arpeggios of the clarinet, the cello makes its appearance, content to point the feeling of the music as a whole. Changes of mood that we in the west more often than not try to disguise are given fuller rein in the less inhibited atmosphere of Slavonic or Magyar music. Thus the slow movement is interrupted by a vigorous, highly dramatic episode in minor tonality. When the opening paragraph is restated it is with new colouring: three horns above cellos and basses. And then the cello, *quasi cadenza*, discourses with the woodwind, until, catching the voice of the persistent flutes, it resolves the movement with distantly beautiful harmonies.

Three horns and string basses. We meet them again in the finale, this time to preface the militant tune which is the focal point of the movement and which the cello introduces at bar 33. Until a change of time at bar 281 this motiv, now reaching towards more impassioned rhythmic utterance, is dominant; but at the *moderato* a second, plaintively beautiful theme (in G major, but nostalgic) is set in the cello to the accompaniment of the faithful clarinets and bassoons. Thereafter are striking alterations of key and B major becomes prominent, in which visions, including one (bar 481) of the *grandioso* theme of the first movement, are conjured up. But at the end it is *allegro vivo* and the rondo finishes with spirited geniality.

⁊ ELGAR · It may very well have been Dvořák's cello concerto that stimulated Elgar to a similar composition. As a young man Elgar had played the violin in the Three Choirs Festival Orchestra, under Dvořák's conductorship, and the first thrill of Dvořák's music never entirely left him. Later in life he came also to admire the playing of the Bohemian Quartet, of which the cellist was Hanuš Wihan. It was for Wihan that Dvořák had composed his concerto.

Elgar's concerto was virtually his swan song. Written in the summer of 1919, in Sussex, it was the last work he composed before the death of Lady Elgar. It was given its first performance in the autumn by Felix Salmond, who later emigrated to America where, as professor of the cello at the Curtis Institute in Philadelphia and of the Juilliard School of Music in New York, he exercised great influence both on playing and on composition.

Elgar's concerto is his most succinct major work, playing only for half an hour. But it is very free in structure. There are four movements: *adagio-moderato*; *allegro molto*; *adagio*; *allegro-moderato–allegro ma non troppo*. The orchestra is as for the violin concerto, but much more sparingly employed. For this is a virtuoso concerto, of which the cello is the supreme arbiter. Thus the soloist, without any introduction, commences the whole work. *Nobilmente*: this, at the outset, recalls the old Elgar. But *nobilmente* is not the prevailing mood either of the movement or of the concerto. It is, rather, pathos. Thus the rather grey pastoral melodies which form the substance of the first movement; the wary manner of the *scherzo*; the lovely intrusion at [66] of the finale of a whole passage which would seem to have been left over from oratorio sketches. It is, however, the slow movement, one long melody, which is the most affecting part of the work. In B flat major it is a hundred miles away from E minor, and a recollection of earlier, happier days—for Elgar was greatly depressed by the war years and the succeeding period of discontent.

From this movement to the slow interlude of Schumann's cello concerto is an easy step; for Schumann, too, recollected earlier joys in an otherwise sombre work. Elgar knew the music of Schumann intimately and the cello concerto shows his Schumann-esque predilections most clearly.

Schumann's concerto is seldom played; largely on account of the orchestration which, devoid of colour, is mostly grey and ghostly. And the solo part, if less ineffective than is often made out, has no commanding public character. But since this is true of most of Schumann's music the cello concerto is by no means uncharacteristic of the composer. Brief—three sections in one movement—it deserves scrutiny on account of the lovely *langsam* section, in which the melodic shapes show the source of some of Elgar's inspiration.

❡ SOME CELLISTS · For obvious reasons—the tonal character, the compass of the instruments, the peculiar problems of scoring —viola and cello concertos have only a modest place in the repertoire. But the cello has been better served than the viola. It had, of course, a place of honour in ensemble music long before the viola, and in the eighteenth century its virtuosi. These, however, were of a homelier order than the violinists and keyboard players. There was, for instance, the long-lived Giacomo Cervetto, who died in 1783 at the age of 101. He played for many years at Drury Lane Theatre—where his solo appearances were affectionately greeted by the groundlings with cries of 'Play up, Nosey'—on account of his appearance. There was also his son James Cervetto, who introduced a cello concerto of Haydn to London in 1784. In Scotland Johann Schetky (1740–1824), who had been cellist to the Landgrave of Hesse-Darmstadt, was a figure of prominence, not only on account of his playing but also because of his friendship with Burns. But the outstanding figure among cellists of that period was Luigi Boccherini, whose technique commanded respect at all the European courts, and whose prolificacy as a composer was remarkable. Of his four cello concertos that in B flat still stands, a little self-consciously, to represent the vogue of the cello in the late eighteenth century.

Cellists would appear conspicuous by their longevity, for Alfredo Piatti (1822–1901) was a familiar and loved figure in English music for more than fifty years. In 1844 Piatti first visited England and fifteen years later he began his long connection with the Popular Concerts. A fine, musicianly player, Piatti was set beside Joachim as a grand exemplar of classical style. It was for Piatti that Sullivan wrote a cello concerto that was performed at the Crystal Palace in 1866; and it was Piatti, too, who gave the first performance in London of Bruch's *Kol Nidrei*—a fine and expressive set of variations for cello and orchestra.

Before Piatti had retired from playing a young Spanish cellist had given his first performance in London: Pau Casals. And here we are in the presence of one who, by his unswerving devotion to the art of music and his subordination of technical skill to musical purpose, has established himself in the twentieth century as venerably as Joachim in the nineteenth.

Besides Casals other notable modern cellists are Suggia, whose portrait by Augustus John gave some visual aid to the popularization of her instrument; Beatrice Harrison; Piatigorsky; Garbusova; and Fournier.

❡ SOME MODERN WORKS · With the re-establishment of the cellist as virtuoso numerous concertos for the instrument have been commissioned. Delius, Milhaud, Khatchaturian, Samuel Barber, Herbert Murrill, are among the composers whose concertos for cello are occasionally heard. But, outside the regular trio of concertos by Dvořák, Schumann, and Elgar, pride of place must probably go to Bloch, whose rhapsody *Schelomo* is a marvellous piece of characterization. Bloch, on whom the influence of Jewish music and tradition is more marked than in the case of any other contemporary composer, chose in *Schelomo* to draw the character of King Solomon; now introspective, now dramatic, now prayerful, now exuberant: a passionate work, which worthily represents a composer of great gifts and noble integrity.

VII. A Miscellany of Concertos

❡ A MATTER OF TIMBRES · We have seen how Mendelssohn, deploring the vulgarity of his Leipzigers, put a damper on natural ebullience, with the result that concert-going became something of a ritual. The solemnity of concert-going is, to some extent, still with us; and humour too often outside the scope of the regulars. Thus the division of music-lovers into the two classes: those who 'know something about it', and those for whom intuition is the only guide. Now any department of musical composition is in itself a continent of experience. There are, within the present study, classical concertos, romantic concertos, concertos which explore nationalism, and so on. The possibilities are endless. But looking at the symphony orchestra the innocent abroad might enquire why—if there are concertos for pianists, violinists (which two groups have the lion's share), violists, and cellists—there do not appear to be many for the other practitioners of instrumental music.

There are two reasons. One, perhaps, is self-evident. There are certain timbres of which the ear tires rather readily. The more intense the tone colour the less one requires of it—as in painting, where also the exotic needs to be handled with discretion. The cor anglais within a score (as, for instance, Berlioz's *Carnaval Romain*) is wonderfully effective; but beyond a certain point the longer it plays the less effective it becomes. So a full-scale concerto, in classical form, becomes impracticable for the cor anglais. And what goes for the cor anglais goes also for the other members of the woodwind and horn families; except, perhaps, the adaptable clarinet, which, chameleon-like, seems able to suit itself to almost any environment.

We return to the old question. What is a concerto? Having by now decided that in a concerto there need not be three movements each patterned according to certain structural precedents, we conclude that concertos of less familiar design might, after all be practicable for the less obvious instruments. Might we not be entertained thereby? And therein lies a quarter, perhaps, of the secret of twentieth-century music. We have joined hands with the eighteenth century, knocked out some of the portentousness of the pedants who, in the wake of the great classical masters, tried to convince us that art was but a form of instruction.

⟦ THE RISE OF THE VIRTUOSO WIND INSTRUMENT PLAYER · There was, it was suggested, another reason for the relative unfamiliarity of concertos for the main body of instrumentalists. It is nearly fifty years since Charles Graves happily noted in the *Spectator* that a testimonial concert was held in honour of Alfred Burnett, who had been for many years a familiar figure in the concert halls of England as an orchestral leader. In the course of his essay Graves summed up the situation of the orchestral player in these words: 'They might . . . not inaptly be compared to leader-writers, in that, like them, they are practically anonymous, and, barring an occasional cadenza or *obbligato* enjoy no opportunity for personal display, but form part of a great organism and express themselves in accordance with the desires and indications of a dictator.' Since that time the situation has somewhat altered and flautists and oboists, clarinettists, bassonists, horn and trumpet players have risen to the instrumental hierarchy.

Within limits a modern wind instrument can play (in the right hands) virtually anything. So much is owed to such men as

Boehm, Lorée, Sax, and many others, who perfected the mechanism of these instruments. Taking all things into consideration then, it is clear that the concerto offers many new tonal attractions. It is also possible at last adequately to realize ambitions of the past. The wind instrument concertos of Mozart (always excepting that for clarinet which is an outstanding musical work in any company) are not among his greatest accomplishments. At the same time, without exception, they illustrate the characters of flute, horn, and bassoon with complete understanding. To what extent the first players surmounted their difficulties is problematic, but in the hands of Gareth Morris, the Brains, Camden, these concertos are irresistible.

❡ WEBER AND OTHER ROMANTIC COMPOSERS · Of the Romantic composers it was Weber who took the deepest interest in the individual qualities of instruments and a number of works for solo instrument and orchestra testify to his interest. In 1811 he composed a concertino and two concertos for Heinrich Bärmann, the famous clarinettist of Munich. The concertino is in one movement, eloquent in its lyrical opening and brilliant in its conclusion. Weber was a master of brilliant tonal effect and his writing for clarinet is not readily surpassable. The bassoon concerto is only less attractive because of the lesser ranges of interest within the instrument. The slow movement, for instance, appears relatively frustrated, but the *giocoso* manner in which the music flits in and out of the shadows in the outside movements is captivating.

Besides the clarinet and bassoon concertos Weber also composed similar works for flute (*Romanza siciliene*) and horn. In all of these works—as in the *divertimenti* of Haydn and Mozart—is idealized the German love of wind music for social occasions.

Interest on the part of the greater composers in wind instruments was spasmodic after Weber. Schumann noted the potentialities of the valve-horn in his little-heard *Concertstück* for four horns and orchestra (Opus 86) and Reinecke, Rheinberger, and Thuille wrote works of varying merit for wind ensembles; while Brahms put the clarinet back into the highest class with his sonata and quintet, written for Richard Mühlfeld.

Of recent years the case has been different. Modern virtuosity
I

has gained its reward, and there is hardly an instrument which has not its own little repertoire of concertos.

Since it was suggested that one might come to know intimately the instruments of the orchestra through concertos, a number of representative modern works are detailed in the order in which the solo instruments are encountered in reading down a page of score.

❡ FLUTE · Among contemporary English-composers Lennox Berkeley is distinguished by a cool, elegant, precise style. So it is that these qualities are happily represented in the flute concerto performed by John Francis at a Promenade Concert in 1953. In this four-movement work the problem of tonal balance is met by reducing the orchestra to chamber proportions, by omitting orchestral flutes, clarinets, and trumpets.

❡ OBOE · If charm is in Berkeley's flute concerto so too it is in the oboe concerto which Richard Strauss composed at the end of his life. When composing Strauss confessed that the themes of his orchestral works came to him already appropriately clad in instrumental colour. The opening theme of the oboe concerto is a beautiful example of a melody that belongs to its instrument. It is an engaging tune midway between art and nature. It is meticulous yet imaginative, as, indeed, is the whole of this work, which is gently scored for small orchestra.

From the beginning of its career the oboe has been associated with pastoral sentiments, and to illustrate this aspect of its nature there is the concerto which Vaughan Williams wrote for Leon Goossens in 1944. A serious work, and of considerable difficulty, it is not, perhaps, among Vaughan Williams's most accessible compositions. But one can be persuaded to the music by fine playing.

❡ CLARINET · Among the woodwind family the clarinet has continued to maintain its supremacy as soloist. One of the most agreeable of clarinet concertos, and unjustifiably neglected, is that by Stanford; an example of his effortless style which, if lacking real originality, is imaginative. Those who are disposed towards music within a temperate climate will also find pleasure in Gerald Finzi's lyrical concerto for clarinet and strings. Such ingratiating works, however, may lead one to false conclusions as to the true character of the instrument. Of recent times the clarinet—especially in the hands of expert dance band musicians—has recaptured some of its former pungency of tone, and to offset latter-day romantic works are two conspicuously original concertos in which the solo instrument plays a more markedly masculine role. These are by the Danish composer Carl Nielsen, and Aaron Copland. In that by Nielsen, a work which represents his great gifts to the full, the clarinet is frequently called from its meditative ranges by the insistent side drum, which is a feature of the score. Copland's concerto was commissioned by Benny Goodman and, not unnaturally, exploits the technique of the jazz player; not that this was an uncongenial undertaking for Copland, who has always been inspired by the belief that music should be for the many and not only for the few, and that it should at all times be aware of popular idiom. The clarinet concerto is a bracing work, owing to Brazilian as well as to American popular music, and even if we may feel that the jazz element becomes a little too self-conscious and the top register tune of the clarinet too conspicuous, of the highest virtuoso order.

❡ BASSOON · The bassoon has gained a reputation for comedy and practically all the old show pieces (with which wind players were formerly content to display their talents at popular concerts) focussed attention on this aspect of personality. But, as Weber demonstrated, there is more to it than this. At the other extreme is a capacity for melancholy, especially in the tenor register, such as is graphically shown in Elgar's *Falstaff*. The greatest of English bassoonists, Archie Camden, has stimulated two concertos—by the Manchester composer Eric Fogg, and by Gordon Jacob. Of these the work by Jacob is the more mature. Relying in this instance on eighteenth-century figuration, and a clean diatonic idiom which is touched with contemporary allusions, he produces a reasonable, well-groomed, if not particularly memorable, concerto. A prolific writer, Jacob has also composed admirable concertos for piano, viola, oboe, horn, and a rhapsody for cor anglais and strings. In each case the scoring is slender.

❡ HORN · Richard Strauss was the son of a horn player in the

Opera orchestra at Munich, and it was to his father Franz that he dedicated his first horn concerto. This Brahmsian piece, written in 1885, in which year Strauss succeeded von Bülow as conductor at Meiningen, is warm, evocative, tuneful; redolent of the summer woodland atmosphere that characterizes so much German romantic writing for this instrument. In 1942 Strauss wrote a second horn concerto, also in the key of E flat, which once was considered the ideal key for horn music. In some ways this work looks back to Mozart, especially in the contour of the horn melodies, in the relationship of keys, and the general character of the movements. There is, however, the characteristic effusiveness of Strauss, and the whole work is both brilliant and warmhearted.

⟮ TRUMPET · The trumpet is not the ideal solo instrument—although, as in the piano concerto of Shostakovich, it forms an admirable foil to a contrasted tone colour—but its claims to concerto status have not been neglected. There is a gay, unpretentious concerto for trumpet, strings, and percussion by John Addison, and a more serious work by Anthony Lewis. Lewis's concerto, performed at a Promenade Concert in 1947, is in effect not a full-scale concerto but an *Elegy* and *Capriccio*.

⟮ TROMBONE; SAXOPHONE; HARP; PERCUSSION; ETC · Concertos for the remaining instruments of the orchestra are mostly and inevitably *jeux d'esprit*. Occupied for some time as an inspector of naval bands, Rimsky-Korsakov composed a concerto for trombone and military band. Otherwise the trombonist, the regal quality of whose instrument has been debased by jazz players, who find in its *cantabile* an aid to reflection, must be content with Gordon Jacob, or Rothmüller's *Divertimento*. Among the puckish pieces of Vaughan Williams's later output are a concerto for tuba (to which instrument the children's choice favourite 'Tubby the Tuba' is the proper introduction) and the *Romance* for harmonica. If the harmonica is thus humoured, why not the accordion? We turn to the *Theme and Variations*, for this instrument and orchestra, by Roy Harris. For saxophone there is an elegant concerto by Phyllis Tate and a characteristically witty *Concertino da camera* by Ibert. This latter, scored only for saxophone and eleven instruments, represents the common modern tendency towards economy and towards the lucidity of the eighteenth century. The harp, with its conventional and commonplace association, is served by William Alwyn in his *Lyra Angelica* and by Norman Dello Joio in his concerto for harp and chamber orchestra: two composers who write without *arrière pensée* and whose works, if not profound, are the source of much ready pleasure. A recent fine concerto by Donatoni for brass and timpani (in which the principal figure is the timpanist), Milhaud's concertos for percussion and strings, and for marimba and vibraphone, and Paul Creston's *Concertino* for marimba and orchestra, effectively demonstrate that in the modern orchestra no instrument need be without its virtuoso pride.

⁋ INFLUENCE OF THE EIGHTEENTH CENTURY · As will have been discovered a large part of modernity is in looking sideways —from 'serious' music to 'light'—and in looking backwards. Romanticism is not likely to perish, but weariness with second-hand idioms has led one composer after another to explore again the wide territory of the baroque period. The concerto is once again an empirical form, in which the guiding principle is no longer a prescribed structural plan, but the contrast of sharply defined tonal qualities. Concertos are now for instruments, and not instruments for concertos.

One obvious result of the baroque revival has been the rehabilitation of the harpsichord. This, not unnaturally, has encouraged the composition of a number of concertos, inevitably shaped after eighteenth-century patterns, among which those by Falla, Milhaud, and Walter Leigh stand out by reason of their modesty, wit, and clarity of expression; virtues derived from the character of the instrument itself.

The eighteenth century has also been responsible for a considerable and important development of interest in the chamber orchestra, whose appearance has frequently been noted in this chapter. Among the works which capture the lucidity of the Age of Reason are Elisabeth Lutyens's *Six Chamber Concertos*, Frank Martin's subtle and beautiful *Petite Symphonie Concertante*, for harpsichord, harp, piano, and double string orchestra, and the same composer's concerto for seven wind instruments.

In nineteenth-century music the harmonic element assumed a preponderant importance. In reaction against this much more recent music has been written with more concentration on the linear aspect; the combination of melodic patterns being conditioned by the character of the individual lines of sound rather than by the exaggerated claims of harmonic theory. Thus the listener should accustom himself to listening, as it were, horizontally. No longer is it a matter of a tune on top, supported by obliging chordal progression; but of appreciating the interweaving of more or less co-equal parts. So we may turn to the vigorous beauty of Michael Tippett's concerto for double string orchestra, an expansive essay in modern counterpoint; to the austere architecture of Vaughan Williams's *Fantasia on a Theme of Thomas Tallis*; to the *Concerto grosso* of Heinrich Kaminski; to the chamber concertos of Hindemith. At which point we are ready to return to the eighteenth century, aware that nothing that is new is not, in some ways, old, and, conversely, that nothing old is not new.

VIII. Bach and Handel

¶ BACH AND THE COURT ORCHESTRA · I have never much appreciated the reverential approach to Bach, inculcated by tribes of teachers to whom counterpoint was a holy mystery, and to be appreciated only by the initiate. Bach was a master craftsman of supreme quality. He possessed immense powers of spiritual perception. But he also had more commonplace virtues, such as led him—sometimes amiably but sometimes with some show of asperity—to accommodate himself to the communities in which he lived. Much of his music—and this is one way to begin to understand it—was a part of this citizenly accommodation. *Gebrauchsmusik* is a term introduced by Paul Hindemith to dignify the occupation of the contemporary composer, who, bending his aspirations according to the requirements of society, writes as and when there is demand for his talents. But Bach, of course, was the great exponent and exemplar of *Gebrauchsmusik*. Thus we may now refer to the Brandenburg concertos, which would hardly have been composed at all had not Bach discovered that such works were needed at the little court of Anhalt-Cöthen. For five years, from 1717 to 1723, he was director of chamber music there.

I take it that there are those whose approach to the music of Bach is cautious. What do we look for? Why is this music different from the music to which we are more generally accustomed? Is some special perception necessary for its appreciation?

Perhaps it is only fair to observe that in general there might be an affirmative answer to the last question. But experience is a better operative word. Orchestral music of the first part of the eighteenth century is not rich in colour as is that of later time. It is not dependent on dynamic subtlety to the same extent. It is less patently 'tuneful', is apparently limited in harmonic range, is rarely exhibitionist. At first, noting these points as apparent deficiencies, we may complain of dullness. 'It is', said the young man who lately set these matters before me in relation to the music of Bach in general, 'all the same.' And this is where he and I began to look at the second of the Brandenburg concertos. This, after all, has a trumpet part of such exciting quality that it must initially gain the respect of all trumpet-philes—whether they have heard of Bach or not. And this is what happened. . . .

❲ INSTRUMENTAL POSSIBILITIES · At Cöthen Bach found not only an orchestra—the normal string group with flutes (both recorders and 'German' flutes), oboes, bassoons, horns, trumpets, and drums—but a prince who was both knowledgeable and especially keen on secular music. Leopold of Anhalt-Cöthen, indeed, was one of a number of eighteenth-century German rulers who participated in the orchestral activities of their courts. Since the court chapel was 'reformed' and therefore devoid of any musical elaboration Bach's primary interest—for the only time in his career—was in instrumental music.

Concerti grossi, especially those of Corelli and Vivaldi, were widely admired at this time and Bach (unlike Handel) took as his model the more vigorous, varied, and progressive Vivaldi. So devoted was Bach to Vivaldi that he adapted some twenty of Vivaldi's concertos to his own needs. And so the form of all

Bach's concertos was that of Vivaldi[1]—three movements; quick, slow, quick. In the Brandenburg concertos he showed an interest akin to that of Vivaldi in all the possible combinations of the instruments at his disposal, and in this respect alone they are fascinating.

In addition to the normal *ripieno* complement of strings and the indispensable harpsichord the Brandenburg concertos show the following *concertino* arrangements: (1) violino piccolo—a small violin with its strings tuned in fifths from middle C upwards, 3 oboes, 2 horns, and bassoon; (2) violin, flute, oboe, trumpet; (4) violin and two flutes; (5) violin and flute, with the harpsichord now elevated to a conspicuous place in the concertino group. That leaves numbers 3 and 6 unaccounted for. In some ways these concertos are the most intriguing of all. For in them the scoring is for strings alone, but with such division of occupation for the players that the result in each case is unrivalled. In the third concerto violins, violas, and cellos are each divided into three, so that from any one group a complete and rich tonal chorus is available. In the sixth concerto violins are entirely excluded and the parts are for 2 violas, 2 viole da gamba (the six-stringed bass member of the viol family, which was eventually supplanted by the cello), cello, and violone (the double-bass of the viol family). In modern performances the viola da gamba and the violone are inevitably replaced by cello and double bass.

❡ QUALITY OF THE MUSIC · At this point one may assist the imagination further by visualizing Bach's instrumentalists settling round him for rehearsal; he at the harpsichord (now more often than not represented by the piano) directing operations. Part of the secret of pleasure in Bach comes from listening, so far as is possible, from within—as though one were taking part in performance. For so much of his output is 'private' music—*musica da camera* in fact, which is sparing in gestures designed to catch the public attention. And as one begins to feel oneself part of the music the matter of counterpoint comes to life. For one is aware of the remarkable division of opportunity, how there is no single

[1] The first Brandenburg Concerto has a number of dance movements added, thus relating to the design of the suite.

part which is not likely not to give satisfaction to the player. Consider, for instance, the bass parts (which at first are easier to follow than middle parts), their athletic properties, and their relation to the whole design. All in all the individual tunes, though proudly independent, are on good terms with each other. It is, to borrow a term from Dr Johnson, 'clubbable' music, conversational and not oratorical. This, perhaps, is why there are those who, without great pretensions to musical knowledge, find that they can live with the concertos of Bach as with the chamber music of Haydn and Mozart.

❡ DESIGN · From the details of scoring we may proceed to the recognition of certain factors of design. These constitute the 'sameness' to which my attention was drawn, but their consistency is no more a hindrance to variety than that to be found in any of the main architectural styles. In all his concertos Bach firmly bases his first movements on the *ritornello* principle. Thus the opening statements will be found to recur at more or less regular intervals in nearly related keys. Such repetitions give strength to the structure. It is as a row of arches in the structure of a building. And the analogy may be carried further. For above and between the arches is space for decoration. So in the concerto of the Bach period, the area between the repetitions of the *ritornello* is occupied by the embellishments of the *concertino*. These, it will be found, grow naturally from the characteristics of the *ritornello* statement. At root the strength of these *ritornellos* is in rhythm. 'It is', Professor Archibald Davidson observes,[1] 'impossible to disassociate rhythm from the remaining substance of Bach's music. The rhythm is, to be sure, a presence vividly felt, but it is so doweled into all the other features that it seems to grow out of them and to be a part of the total structure of the music. It would be impossible to over-emphasize Bach's fondness for strong rhythm.'

Thus the independence of the individual parts in the texture of his concertos and their powerful rhythmic drive present a rare musical vitality—with its own relevance to the spirit of modern times. On consideration it will be agreed that to infect such music

[1] *Bach and Handel: The Consummation of the Baroque in Music* (Harvard 1951); an excellent book.

with the nuances appropriate to the Romantic style would be injudicious.

The outer movements of Bach's concertos (the last is sometimes in the manner of a gigue, or fugal, or according to the first movement scheme) are massive, plain-spoken, but brilliantly intellectual in their contrapuntal interplay. In the slow middle movements there is opportunity for the display of quite other ideas. In these the baroque character prevails; either in long lines of melody, full with notes, or in the spacious disposition of interweaving patterns. See, for example, the oboe melody of the first Brandenburg concerto on the one hand, or the intense counterpoint of flute and violin in the fifth. But there is no strict conformity. The third Brandenburg concerto has no slow movement beyond two chords (which almost certainly were originally embellished by Bach's genius for extemporization), while that of the fourth has all the quality of an excerpt from *Passion* music.

To say that the more one comes to know the Brandenburg concertos the more one loves them has all the appearance of a truism. But it must be pointed out to the impetuous that Bach commands patience, and that when this is exercised appreciation grows apace. From recognizing the excellence of the parts one proceeds to that point when they form a whole within experience. And then one needs not to ask whether or not the music bears a specific meaning.

As well as the Brandenburg concertos Bach also wrote his violin concertos (including that in D minor for two violins) at Cöthen.

❡ AT LEIPZIG · In Leipzig he included among his duties the conductorship of the *Collegium Musicum*, a society principally maintained for the benefit of students of the university, from among whom the orchestra was chiefly enlisted. Weekly meetings —out of doors in the summer and in Gottfried Zimmermann's coffee house during the winter months—called for a good deal of music. Faced with the task of providing it Bach turned again to some of his Cöthen music. In his violin concertos in E major and A minor he saw further possibilities, and re-arranged them with the harpsichord now taking the place of the solo violin. The fourth

Brandenburg concerto also became a concerto for solo harpsichord and strings, while various movements from church cantatas furnished the material for yet another. Of the remaining clavier concertos those in D minor and F minor may also have been transcribed from violin concertos now no longer extant; but there is, despite the apparent string figuration of some of the keyboard writing, an even chance that they were designed in the first place for the medium in which they are now known. These, for all practical purposes, are, in any case, the earliest of clavier concertos.

In the fifth of the Brandenburg concertos Bach allowed himself much latitude in the clavier part. Sixty-six bars of clavier alone precede the final orchestral tutti of the first movement—an exciting entertainment for nimble fingers. But, it might be thought, there is rather too much of it. In the clavier concertos such exuberance is not permitted, for cadenzas as such are mostly disallowed. But in that in D minor there are moments in the first and last movements where the solo instrument asserts its power in brief but pregnant unaccompanied flourishes. Of these the most impressive is the last—before the final *tutti* of the whole work—where a great climax is achieved by the unexpected intermission of a noble *adagio* bar. Nobility lies also in the slow movement—a piece built on a ground bass, which was used in another context as the opening chorus of the Church Cantata No. 146.

As well as these solo concertos Bach wrote some for more than one clavier. There are two in C minor for two claviers, which were adapted from violin concertos. And for the same medium is a concerto in C major, which would appear to have been originally written in its present form. Of this the last movement is very nearly the most exhilarating fugue ever written. The two concertos for three claviers are commonly thought to have been family pieces. At one keyboard was Bach himself. At the others his sons Carl Philipp Emanuel (whose E flat concerto for harpsichord and 'fortepiano' deserves mention both for its intrinsic charm and its transitional instrumentation) and Wilhelm Friedemann. Finally there is yet another adaptation of a work by Vivaldi in the concerto for four claviers.

❡ HANDEL IN LONDON · In his own day Bach was no more than a provincial notability. Handel, on the other hand, was essentially metropolitan: a great public figure in a world of fashion and sophistication. Within the orchestral music of Bach lies something of the quality of the life and thought of Cöthen and Leipzig. In that of Handel there is less of intimacy and much more consciousness of the necessity for public attributes. There may obviously be instanced the *Water Music* and the *Music for the Royal Fireworks*, which (see the disposition of the wind parts) are of *concerto grosso* provenance.

When a suite[1] of *Water Music* pieces was performed on 17 July 1717, the barge which was assigned to the musicians carried a band of fifty players. And when, thirty-two years later, the Peace of Aix-la-Chapelle was celebrated with a display of fireworks, and with Handel's ceremonial music, the wind band (Handel added strings to his score for subsequent performances in the Chapel of the Foundling Hospital and elsewhere) was more than fifty strong. Necessarily broad effects were the order of the day, and with their result Handel was not disappointed. For at the rehearsal in Vauxhall Gardens an eager crowd of 12,000 was patently delighted.

For many years the music of Handel was one of the chief attractions of the pleasure gardens opened by Jonathan Tyers in 1732 in Vauxhall. And those who approved the erection there of a statue in honour of Handel's association with the place represented all sections of London society. Excerpts from operas and oratorios titillated the ears of amorous apprentices and their masters, of timid maid-servants and their mistresses. And sometimes they reflected on the majesty of Handel's music. It was not only in the nineteenth century that this property was recognized. Nor was it necessary to have prodigious companies of performers. The organ concertos were for a very small instrument, with few stops and no pedals, with strings, oboes, and bassoons. And yet this was the effect of one of them on the author of a vivid

---

[1] The music left by Handel and entitled *Water Music* fell into two groups of pieces, one in F major, the other in D major; from which it would seem that originally there were two separate suites which were played on different occasions. The Boosey and Hawkes score contains nine pieces, arranged concerto-grosso-wise, from the F major group.

pen picture of London life entitled *The Foundling Hospital of Wit* (1743):

❡ ORGAN CONCERTOS · '. . . at the Sound of the Organ my Soul danced for Joy; and the Man's Finger, that played upon the Organ, was a cunning Finger.

'And there was great Harmony betwixt the Sound of the Organ, and the Sound of the other Instruments; and it happened, that whatever the Organ on one Side spake, the Fiddles on the other Side cry'd, "So say we". This also pleased me.

'Albeit there was not heard the Voice of Singing-men, or of Singing-women, and the Music lacked Interpretation.

'And I said, How wot I now what is piped or harped? Verily this is as it were sounding Brass, or a tinkling Cymbal.'

Perhaps if the author had gone to the oratorio performances of Handel he would have discovered some particular significance in the organ concertos, for they were introduced by Handel as entractes between the parts of the oratorios (the fine overture to *Saul* is, as it stands, virtually an organ concerto). Twelve concertos were issued in two sets in 1738 (Op. 4) and 1740 respectively. A third set of six (Op. 7) was published posthumously. The second set, comprising arrangements—mostly of the *concerti grossi* (Op. 6), is of less consequence than the others. But in Op. 4 and Op. 7 there is a great deal of Handel at his best; lithe music, expressing the incomparable Handelian *joie de vivre* and the *joie de jouer* that is characteristic of all his keyboard music and which makes these particular works pioneers in the solo concerto, and deliciously balanced in regard to the contrasting activities of organ and strings. Within their tonal limits (in addition to strings there are oboes and bassoons) is a wealth of instrumental colour; the opening of Op. 7, No. 4, will serve as an eloquent example. And each work is a law unto itself in the matter of form. So there are movements in *ritornello* style, in fugal manner, on ground basses (Op. 7, Nos. 1 and 5), or in dance forms. But, alas, missing from the extant scores is much at which we may only guess. *Organo ad libitum*: the direction is frequent. At such points Handel would extemporize. Of his style in playing his concertos we have the testimony of Sir John Hawkins:

❡ STYLE IN PLAYING · 'When he gave a Concerto, his method in general was, to introduce it with a Voluntary movement on the Diapasons, which stole on the ear in a slow and solemn progression; the harmony closely wrought, and as full as could possibly be expressed; the passages constructed with stupendous art; the whole, at the same time, being perfectly intelligible, and having the appearance of great simplicity. This kind of prelude was succeeded by the Concerto itself, which he executed with a degree of spirit and firmness that no one even pretended to equal.' In which lie the directions for those who would interpret Handel: with simplicity, with spirit, with firmness.

❡ GRAND CONCERTOS · But these organ concertos (the only works in which organ and orchestra have ever been happily mated) may easily be destroyed by the inflationary process which forces into the original scoring opportunities for alien brass and woodwind. Not so, fortunately, the 'grand' concertos of Op. 6, which were composed in 1739. For these works the model was Corelli, whom Handel had known in Rome thirty years previously. But Handel wrote with a breadth of experience that Corelli did not have, so that within these twelve concertos it is as though the whole of humanity is under scrutiny. Ideas and personalities are epitomized in melodies which are unfailingly memorable in themselves—in contrast to those of Bach which demand expansion through the dialectic of his design. Of these concertos of Handel two may be taken as representative.

In No. 3, in E minor, the first movement is a *larghetto*, in which *concertino* and *ripieno* instruments are occupied with a four-bar phrase of grave dignity. Ending not on a tonic but on a dominant chord this leads to an *andante*. Here it seems that Handel is aware of his German origins; for there is poignancy in the shape of the first violin tune and tension in the counter-tune which is played by the second violins. This is music which Bach would have understood. So too is that of the following *allegro*, a rough piece akin to the Brandenburg *allegro* movements in design but much less complex in the *concertino* interludes. Handel's simplicity, however, should not be misunderstood. A six-bar episode can stir infinite speculation. So we meet at bar 22 a sequential passage wherein the strings are playing in octaves; but now in G major, now in A minor, and now in B minor. From such brusqueness Handel turns to delicacy in a Polonaise (c.f. the Polacca of the first Brandenburg concerto) in G major. Finally there is a short piece in which there are delightful alternations between *concertino* and *ripieno*, and in which the original key of E minor is re-established.

That Handel sometimes deals in thunderbolts is well understood. His tenderness is, perhaps, less familiar. Yet—as shown in the greatest degree in *Theodora* and *Jephtha*—this is at the heart of his genius. Therefore the sixth concerto of Op. 6 is to be recommended on account of the third movement *musette*. In this there is affection in every bar. In the preceding movements there are dramatic points in the preludial *larghetto*, and a fine example of Handel's fugal style in the *allegro ma non troppo*. After the *musette* is an *allegro* in which the concertino is reduced to a solo violin; and, finally, a graceful dance in triple time, in which one is reminded of the cosmopolitan quality of Handel. For here is the French influence which came from Lully to England through Purcell.

The concertos of Bach and Handel are not what immediately and loosely we consider concertos ought to be. But having read thus far it will have been discovered that the crux of the matter is 'playing together'. From which principle has emerged indispensable music. And this is what matters.

IX. Some Aspects of Interpretation

❡ WHAT WE EXPECT · A trumpeter of my acquaintance called
in one day to excuse himself from an engagement, on account of
a tempting contract from a foreign recording company to take
part in a performance of Bach's second Brandenburg concerto—
a high spot for trumpeters, as has already been indicated. On his
return I enquired as to the success of his mission. 'Wonderful',
he enthused, 'a perfect performance!' Not unnaturally this was a
partial point of view, and further enquiry showed how imperfect
can be perfection. When recording, and out of consideration for
the trumpeter, the work was split, more or less arbitrarily, into
small sections; so that the trumpeter having got eight bars right
could relax over a cup of coffee before tackling the next passage.
Finally, of course, the tapes were composed into a complete concerto. So may science triumph over art. But not in this way can
a valid interpretation be achieved.

Which brings us to what we expect. A proper concerto, according to my young and not altogether discriminating friends, gives
scope to the virtuoso, and that is its main end. Nor is this attitude
quite unreasonable, for there is no concerto (not even the *concerti*

grossi of Corelli and Handel) which does not in some degree intend virtuosity. On the other hand this is not the sole quality of a concerto.

The necessarily fine and complicated structure of such a work, the prevailing imaginative mood of a great concerto, both indicate other factors. We must, then, anticipate contrast—as between solo and tutti passages; a capacity for subordination—when the orchestra is used as pure accompaniment, as in the slow movement of Mendelssohn's violin concerto, or when the soloist is thus engaged as in the middle section of César Franck's *Symphonic Variations*; and a mutual understanding between soloist and conductor.

⟨ THE CONDUCTOR · The performance of a concerto is a challenge both to soloist and conductor, for each has to accept a measure of dual control. Particularly, however, it is the conductor who is required most to reorientate himself, for opportunities of impressing his own 'interpretation' on both the chosen work and the audience are somewhat limited. For once his majesty is tempered by the presence of another attraction on the steps of the throne! And successfully to present a concerto demands more of time and patience in rehearsal than symphony or tone poem.

But we may easily have misconceptions about the profession of conductor. What should be his background? Charles Münch gives the answer to this in his autobiographical *I am a Conductor*.[1] A conductor, he urges from his own experience in the Leipzig Gewandhaus orchestra under Furtwängler, should have been trained first as an orchestral player. Rudolph Dolmetsch, in his *Art of Orchestral Conducting*,[2] further requires that he who would conduct concertos should have proved himself in either pianoforte accompaniment or chamber music playing—or both. Not every conductor arrives at his destination by these routes, but if in his handling of the concerto situation he appears so to have done then we should be satisfied. One who has been an orchestral player (Barbirolli) has a natural inclination to selectivity of timbre, so that the appropriate tone colour is generally persuaded from the ensemble. One who has been an efficient and successful

[1] New York, London, 1955.   [2] London, 1942.

accompanist (Sargent) instinctively knows how phrases shared between soloist and orchestra should be made to match, how sections should be dovetailed, and how much liberty is permissible to a soloist. An ex-chamber-music-player (Blech) might well be expected to effect clarity of utterance, such as is indispensable, for instance, in playing Mozart.

⁋ REQUIREMENTS OF THE CONDUCTOR · Balance of tone; clarity; blend of sonorities: these are the clear essentials of a good performance. Immediately, the first means that the solo instrument and the orchestra shall not impede each other, and obviously it is the orchestra that stands in greatest danger of transgression. In Tchaikovsky's first piano concerto the piano looks after itself pretty well, despite a frequent massing of orchestral resources against it, but in Beethoven's fourth piano concerto, or Schumann's cello concerto—to take only two convenient examples— it is very easy to fall into one of two errors. Either the accompaniment dominates by being not more than a fraction beyond the possible limit, or it is so discreet as to lose its rhythmic point. It is only the conductor who can achieve the properly balanced relationship.

Clarity implies lucidity both of line and texture. The *locus classicus* might well be Mozart's piano concerto in A major (K. 488). Each quaver and semiquaver in this work has its own right to be heard, and any tendency towards speed for its own sake puts notes of these denominations under sentence of extinction. In the same score there are many occasions when the piano and a pair of woodwind instruments are co-equal, and if this is not noticed by the conductor the luminosity of the performance is impaired. As for blending sonorities the concertos of Beethoven, in which the departments of the orchestra converge and diverge, now in the background, now in the foreground, may be studied. Or almost any modern concerto —such as the violin concerto of Bartók, or the viola concerto of Walton—will show how perceptive must be the conductor's ear.

With these points in mind we proceed to the larger virtues. 'Before setting himself to work . . . the conductor must be in possession of a rhythmic plan of the performance' (Lazare

Saminsky). 'The conductor's instinct would obviously, if he is intelligent, lead him to bear in mind the epoch, literary implications, and form of the composition' (Sir Malcolm Sargent).[1] From these observations it is clear that the conductor must be able to see whatever he conducts as a unity. Needless to say he must be able through his technique to make his audience aware of this unity also.

Now a concerto is one of the most thrilling experiences in music. Not for the obvious reason, which comes first to mind and has been already mentioned; but because in general it is so exclusively musical. Symphonies fairly often wander away to speculate on literature or some other non-musical subject; concertos hardly ever. Thus the interpreter of integrity can devote his whole attention to the quality and significance of the music itself. The listener may here ask himself if he loses any pleasure in music because the great concertos bear no descriptive titles. (That of the 'Emperor' is, as has been seen, both unauthorized and irrelevant.)

❡ THE SPIRIT OF THE COMPOSER · Sir Malcolm Sargent asks that in relation to a composition the epoch should be borne in mind. When this is done in a detailed way the results may be startling to the conventional music-lover. Handel's organ concertos played on a baroque chamber organ; harpsichords and recorders re-asserting themselves in the works of Bach; bows specially constructed after the eighteenth-century pattern for the performance of Corelli; a forte-piano in Mozart: is this what 'bearing in mind the epoch' means? To some, obviously, it does, and their endeavours to maintain standards of accuracy may well stimulate new pleasure; even if one wonders how much of the known incompetence of some eighteenth-century performers should be reintroduced to give an even clearer idea of the original. But there are others, less musicologically minded, who contrive to play Bach on the piano and still appear to present adequately the 'spirit of the composer', and of his age.

A composition, it may be said, never really reaches the ideal state in which it once existed in the composer's mind, for nota-

[1] Quoted from *The New Art of Conducting*, Lazare Saminsky (London 1957)

tion is limiting and fallible. Thus it is that in re-creating a work
from the score the artist must inevitably interpret according to
his conception of the original idea. There is, then, some room
for manoeuvre; for variation in *tempo*; for range in dynamics; for
imperceptible lengthening or accentuation of notes (as shown by
Bruno Walter in his recorded rehearsal of Mozart's 'Linz' symphony). But not too much. In one set of records of the Mozart
violin concertos in my possession the soloist, distinguished in
other fields than the Mozartian, lards the innocence of his line
with an unctuous sentimentality which belongs neither to Mozart
nor to his epoch. There are other recordings which send Bach's
clavier concertos stampeding into the world as though in hot
pursuit of Tchaikovsky. On the other hand a wrong kind of
'correctness' frequently denies to Elgar the flexibility which his
style so earnestly requests.

⟨ THE SOLOIST · Of all this the conductor should be aware, and
also the soloist. Any performer must be subject to a stern self-
discipline; but some are not conspicuous in this respect. So that
lassitude is sometimes confused with 'soulfulness', so that slow
movements may very well go slower and slower, until the conductor, sometimes a little spitefully, applies a dose of strict time;
in which case neither the freedom nor the discipline is acceptable,
because they are not related, either to one another or anything else.

The severest test for a soloist (for here is a great temptation)
may well be the cadenza. As has been seen, since the time of
Mendelssohn composers have tried to make this baroque feature
non-extrusive, by means of supporting accompaniment or by
well-controlled thematic reference. In classical concertos, however, the cadenza has often been regarded as a field-day for the
performer which he must enjoy to the full. So a cadenza badly
handled—which is not the same as badly played—may sound like
a movement within a movement. One may admire the skill, but
in so doing forget the course of the music as a whole.

It is axiomatic that the conductor should envisage a work as a
whole, and in respect of a concerto it is not less imperative that
the solo performer should make clear a comparable understanding. On the purely mechanical level he (or she) must give the im-

pression of being involved in the music even when not playing, so that when fresh entries are made they should seem to grow out of the preceding argument of the *tutti*. To effect such exchange is no easy matter, and cool judgment and sensitivity are called for.

Above the technical level, however, lies the emotional and intellectual. It is here that the artist's real quality shows itself. Most competent players produce the right notes, but more than competence is called for if they are to be delivered in a compelling manner. Concertos, as other large works in music, range widely in emotional colour, and the performer must realize this in subtle shades of nuance, in variety of tone, in exposition of rhythmic subtleties, and so on. But the variety of expression must be unified so that the listener is aware of an integrated personality within the music: the 'spirit of the composer' in fact.

So we may approach the best critics with some appreciation of their insight. (A critic, being usually neither conductor nor performer by trade, is the ordinary listener raised, sometimes, to a higher degree.) When one reads that Ruggiero Ricci 'gives a very fine performance [of Tchaikovsky's violin concerto], deeply musical and without any striving after effect', or of Edwin Fischer's recording of the 'Emperor' that 'he shows a marked concern for beauty of tone . . . but [that there is] a certain lack of the scale and vigour proper to this glorious work, and the last movement is deficient in muscular tension', it is easy to see what Desmond Shawe-Taylor means to convey. The former performance is unified and therefore satisfying, the latter exquisite in certain aspects, but deficient in the contrast essential to a rounded interpretation.

❡ THE ORCHESTRA · More often than not the function of the orchestral player is taken for granted; soloist and conductor tending to monopolize attention. It is worth listening to a familiar concerto once or twice with the ear trained particularly on the orchestral part. If it has not already been noticed the complexity of this part will cause surprise. The slow movement of Elgar's violin concerto will show as well as anything the care which each individual instrumentalist must take if the result is to be at all adequate. The soloist can demonstrate the temper of his interpretation; the conductor can coax or browbeat (if there is time in the rehearsal); but unless each member of the orchestra feels a personal responsibility the likelihood of an inspiring—as distinct from a competent—performance is remote. A great personality such as was Furtwängler could inspire rank and file players so that they felt themselves in no inferior situation. Thus a Beethoven concerto conducted by Furtwängler is normally characterized by the richness and significance of the orchestral part. It is the same with great piano accompanists; their superlative art should make one ashamed to use the subordinate term accompanist. Great conductors, like great accompanists, however, are rare, and so it is that one must be too often satisfied, especially in concertos, with merely adequate playing.

⁋ THE LISTENER · For this the listener must share some responsibility. The glamorized lady pianist, the eminent, immaculate, infallible conductor—so represented at least by garish journalism —invite curiosity or affection. But without the long-suffering orchestra they are helpless. So one must learn to listen rather than to look, and to listen to concertos as a whole. To listen to a concerto as a whole: that is the essence of musical understanding.

INDEXES

Index of Works and Recordings

The following index gives publishers and selected long-playing recordings of the principal works mentioned in the text. Publishers are abbreviated thus (italic type denotes that a miniature score is available):

A, Augener
B & H, Boosey and Hawkes
Br., Breitkopf
C, Chester
D, Durand
E, Eulenberg
F, Carl Fischer
L, Lengnick

N, Novello
OUP, Oxford University Press
R, Ricordi
Sa, Salabert
Sch, Schott
Si, Simrock
U, Universal
W, Joseph Williams

     [1] Which is what the pianoforte was formerly called.

---

[1] Not yet available in U.K.
[2] Long out of print and therefore difficult to come by, but to be published
in a new edition of the works of Field in the series *Musica Britannica*.

[1] Agents for Anglo-Soviet Music Press Ltd.

LALO, Eduard (1823–92),
> *Symphonie espagnole*, Op. 21, for vl. & orch.; *E*; Columbia 33CX 1246
> *Concerto russe*, Op. 29, for vl. & orch.; Schirmer
> *Fantaisie norvégienne*, for vl. & orch.; Bote

LAMBERT, Constant (1905–51),
> *Rio Grande*, for pfte., chorus, & orch.; *OUP*; Columbia 33SX1003
> Concerto for pfte. & 9 instr.; OUP; Argo RG 50

LEIGH, Walter (1905–42), Concertino for harpsichord & str.; OUP

LEWIS, Anthony (b. 1915), Concerto for tr. & orch.; L

LIEBERMANN, Rolf (b. 1910), Concerto for jazz band & symph. orch.; *U*

LISZT, Franz (1811–86),
> Concertos for pfte. & orch.:
>> no. 1 in E flat; *B & H*; HMV BLP 1013
>> no. 2 in A; *E*; Columbia 33CX1106
> *Todentanz* for pfte. & orch.; *E*; Parlophone PMD 1026

LOEFFLER, Charles (1861–1935),
> *Pagan Poem*, Op. 14, for pfte. & orch.; Schirmer; Capitol CTL 7033

LUTYENS, Elisabeth (b. 1906), Six Chamber Concertos, Op. 8; C[1]

MARTIN, Frank (b. 1890),
> Concerto for 7 wind instr.; U
> *Petite symphonie concertante*; *U*; Decca LXT 2631

MENDELSSOHN, Felix (1809–47),
> Concertos for pfte. & orch.:
>> no. 1 in G. mi., Op. 25; *E*; Vox PL 7440
>> no. 2 in D mi., Op. 40; A; Nixa PLP 229
> Concerto in E mi., Op. 64, for vl. & orch.; *B & H*; Vox PL 8840
> *Serenade and allegro giojoso*, Op. 43, for pfte. & orch.; A
> *Capriccio brillant*, Op. 22, for pfte. & orch.; A; Decca LXT 2932
> *Rondo brillant*, Op. 29, for pfte. & orch.; A; Decca LXT 2932

MILHAUD, Darius (b. 1892),
> Concertos for cello and orch. (nos. 1[2] & 2); *Sa*
> Concerto for perc. & small orch.; U; Capitol CTL 7094
> Concerto for marimba & vibraphone & orch.; Enoch[3]
> *L'Apothéose de Molière*; suite for harpsichord & str.; unpublished.

MOERAN, Ernest (1894–1950), Concerto in D for vl. & orch.; N

MOSCHELES, Ignaz (1794–1870),
> 'Fantastic' Concerto, no. 6, for pfte. & orch.; Schlesinger
> 'Pathetic' Concerto, no. 7, for pfte. & orch.; Schlesinger

---

[1] Nos. 1 and 3 in min. score.
[2] Recorded (with no. 1 of Prokofiev) by Janos Svarkev, but not yet available in U.K.
[3] Also arranged as *Suite concertante*, for pfte. & orch., which is available in min. score.

Mozart, Wolfgang (1756–91),

    Concertos for pfte. & orch.:

        in B flat, K 456; *E*; Vox PL 8300

        in D mi., K 466; *E*; Vox PL 8430

        in A, K 488; *E*; Decca LXT 2867

        in C mi., K 491; *E*; Vox PL 6880

        in C, K 503; *E*; Columbia 33SX 1044

    Concerto in F for 3 pfte. & orch., K 242; Br

    Concertos for vl. & orch.:

        in B flat, K 207; *B & H*; Columbia 33SV 1017

        in D, K 211; *E*; Nixa PLP 549

        in G, K 216; *E*; Nixa WLP 5187

        in D, K 218; *E*; Philips ABL 3040

        in A, K 219; *E*; Nixa WLP 5187

    Concerto in G for fl. & orch.; K 313; *E*; Philips ABL 3059

    Concerto in D for fl. & orch.; K 314; *E*; Vox PL 8130

    Concerto in A for clar. & orch., K 622; *B & H*; Brunswick AXL 2002

    Concerto in B flat for bassoon & orch., K 191; *E*; Vox PL 8870

    Concertos for horn & orch.:

        in D. K 124;

        in E flat, K 417;

        in E flat, K 447;   } *E*; Columbia 33CX 1140

        in E flat, K 495;

    Symphonia concertante for vl., vla., & orch.; K 364; *B & H*; Vox PL 7320

Murrill, Herbert (1909–1952),

    Concerto no. 1 for cello & orch.; OUP

    Concerto no. 2, 'El cant dels ocells', for cello & orch.; OUP

Nielsen, Carl (1884–1931),

    Concerto for clar. & orch., Op. 57; Dania, Copenhagen; Decca LXT 2979

Paganini, Niccolo (1782–1840),

    Concerto no. 1 in D, Op. 6, for vl. & orch.; R; Vox PL 6490

    Concerto no. 2 in B mi., Op. 7, for vl. & orch.; R; Nixa BLP 1018

Prokofiev, Sergei (1891–1953),

    Concerto no. 3 for pfte. & orch., Op. 26; *B & H*; Decca LXT 2894

Rachmaninov, Sergei (1873–1943),

    Concertos for pfte. & orch.:

        no. 1 in F sharp mi., Op. 1; *B & H*; HMV CLP 1037

        no. 2 in C mi., Op. 18; *B & H*; HMV CLP 1007

    Rhapsody on a Theme of Paganini, for pfte. & orch.; *Sch.*; Decca LXT 2862

Ravel, Maurice (1875–1937),

    Concerto in G for pfte. & orch.; *D*; Decca LXT 2816

    Concerto for pfte. (left hand) & orch.; *D*; Decca LXT 2816

L

I wish to acknowledge the assistance of Mr L. W.
Duck, of the Henry Watson Music Library, in
compiling this index.

General Index

Addinsell, Richard, 89
Addison, John, 132
Adler, Larry, 25
Alwyn, William, 133
Amadei, Filippo, 34 fn.
Amati family, 30
Aranyi, Jelly d', 113
Armstrong, Louis, 12
Arnold, Matthew, 50
Artôt, Désirée, 83
Auer, Leopold, 107

Bach, Carl Philipp Emanuel, 36, 140
Bach, Johann Sebastian, 14, 26, 34, 35, 36, 37, 40, 65, 78, 92, 117, 135–40, 141, 143, 144, 145, 148
Bach, John Christian, 36, 37
Bach, Wilhelm Friedemann, 140
Balakirev, Mily, 80
Barber, Samuel, 126
Barbirolli, John, 113, 146
Bärmann, Heinrich, 129
Barry, Mme du, 36
Bartók, Béla, 25; 42, 92-4, 115–17, 121, 147
Bax, Arnold, 25, 112, 119
Beethoven, Ludwig van, 14, 25, 39–40, 42, 50, 54, 55–62, 64, 65, 66, 70 71, 147, 151

Benedict, Julius, 41
Bennett, Robert Russell, 27
Berg, Alban, 42, 117
Berkeley, Lennox, 130
Berlioz, Hector, 22, 40, 41, 68, 76, 115, 118–19, 121, 128
Blech, Harry, 147
Bliss, Arthur, 98, 99–100, 112, 114–15
Bloch, Ernest, 41, 106, 110, 121, 126
Blom, Eric, 81
Boccherini, Luigi, 25, 45, 125
Boehm, Theobald, 129
Borodin, Alexander, 80
Boult, Adrian, 99
Brahms, Johannes, 18, 22, 24, 25, 42, 62–6, 77, 78, 92, 103, 106, 107, 115, 121
Brain family, 129
Britten, Benjamin, 17
Brodsky, Adolf, 107
Browning, Robert, 23
Bruch, Max, 108, 125
Bülow, Hans von, 132
Burnett, Alfred, 128
Burns, Robert, 125
Byron, Lord, 118

Camden, Archie, 25, 129, 131
Campoli, Alfredo, 114, 115

163

Date Due

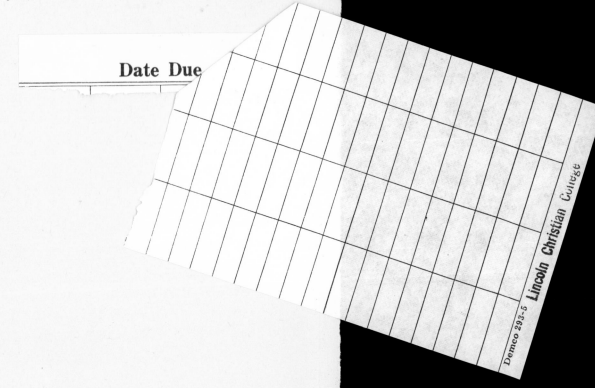